Writing Is Learning

Strategies for Math, Science, Social Studies, and Language Arts

Howard Wills

EDINFO
PRESS

Wills, Howard.
  Writing is learning: strategies for math, science, social studies, and
  language arts / Howard Wills.
      p. cm.
  Includes bibliographical references.
  ISBN 1-883790-00-X : $14.95
  1. English language--Composition and exercises--Study and teaching--
United States. 2. Interdisciplinary approach in education--United States.
I. Title.
  LB1576.W4887 1993
  372.6'23--dc20   93-29262
                                                          CIP

EDINFO Press
P.O. Box 5247
Bloomington, Indiana 47407

CONTENTS

PREFACE vii

ACKNOWLEDGMENTS ix

INTRODUCTION xi
   Different Writing for Different Purposes xii
   Reflective/Expressive Writing xiii
   The Organization of this Book xiv
   One Student's Thoughts on Writing xvii

1 GETTING STARTED
  Journals and Learning Logs 1
   Keeping a Journal: A Personal Experience 2
   Journal Entries 5
   Unprompted Journal Writing 8
      Young Learners Write 14
      Supporting Student Writing 16
   Prompted Journal Writing 17

Prompts for Young Learners 19
Using the Short Story for Learning 21
Legitimate Concerns of English Teachers..... 23
Dialogue Journals.. 24
Coaching instead of Teaching 26
Sharing Thoughts about Books 30
Using These Activities in Your Classroom.......... 33

2 PUTTING IDEAS IN ORDER
Narratives and Problem Solving 37

Narratives: Real-World Applications 38
Peer Dialogues: Letters 43
Letters to Aliens.. 46
Role Playing 49
Scriptwriting: Radio Reporter 49
Real-Life Roles 51
Chemical Company Executive 52
Concerned Citizen 54
Writing about Problem Solving 55
Structured Explanation 56
Simple Explanation 61
Less Time Reteaching 63
Using These Activities in Your Classroom.......... 65

3 BECOMING MORE SPECIFIC
Definitions and Reviews...67

Extended Definitions 69
Natural and Unthreatening 75
Book Reviews/Reading Letters 76
Teacher's Comments 81
Peer Review and Response 83
Protocol for Peer Review and Response 84
Mutually Reinforcing Skills 84
Actual Student Responses 86
Using These Activities in Your Classroom.......... 88

Twenty (Better) Questions for Your
Reading Letter 90
Form for Reading Letter 92
Guidelines for Extended Definitions 93
Checklist for Writing Extended Definition
Essay 94

4 ORGANIZING INFORMATION
Summaries 97
Reading Summaries 98
More Practice Writing Summaries 102
Learning Summaries 102
Field Notes from the Future 108
Note Taking 111
Focused Freewriting 113
Purposes for Using Focused Freewriting 113
Essays 116
Using These Activities in Your Classroom 121

5 SUMMING UP
Letter Writing 123
How Do I Use Writing to Learn? 125
Benefits to Students 128
Benefits to Teachers 130
Using These Activities in Your Classroom 133

EPILOGUE 135

REFERENCES 139

PREFACE

For some of us, learning and writing are natural working companions. When we are studying or learning, we have a pen in hand. When we are trying to figure out problems in life or in school, we start by jotting down our ideas and the steps we might take. Perhaps that's the reason that "writing across the curriculum" to me is an answer, not a question.

In today's world of schooling, one of the fundamental principles calls for students to become directly involved in their own learning. What better way to encourage that principle than to ask students to make visible their own thinking processes by writing? As students set goals or purposes, examine the content of their own minds, determine how to get meaning from their work, and then bring a learning experience to a satisfactory resolution, they need to make their thoughts visible so they can play with them. Once on paper (or on the computer screen), thoughts can be moved, changed, revisited, and discarded. But first, the learner has to see what he or she is dealing with.

The teacher's role in an environment where students shape and pursue their own learning goals is to provide direction, resources, and the tools or skills that the learner needs. That's one of the major reasons for this book and its personality, that is, a reporter's approach to what some teachers and students are doing to use writing as a significant vehicle for learning. This book shows teachers and students in the process of making thoughts visible for various learning purposes.

When Howard Wills, journalist and writing teacher, finished ERIC's inservice staff development program on **Writing across the Curriculum,** I asked him to write a book that could be distributed to all teachers, a book that would demonstrate writing as a learning vehicle rather than philosophize about the beauty of integrated learning. He accepted that challenge and using his journalism background leaped right into the midst of classrooms where teachers and students were already writing to learn, not writing to produce a written composition.

This book will serve all subject teachers who want ideas and examples for using writing in their classrooms, and it will give administrators glimpses of classrooms where students are indeed actively involved in their own learning.

Carl B. Smith, Director
ERIC Clearinghouse on Reading,
English, and Communication

ACKNOWLEDGMENTS

Many individuals cooperated in a cheerful and timely manner in the production of this text. Writing, indeed, is a social act. I want to thank Carl Smith at Indiana University who conceived this project and whose attention and experience were generously offered—and gratefully accepted. Jerome Harste and Larry Mikulecky at Indiana University also supported this work in more ways than I can say, as did Jacqueline Franz of IUPUI-Columbus, and Darlene. Susan Moke merits special recognition and thanks for contributing editing skills nonpareil.

To my friends in Kentucky—the inspiring teachers, administrators, and students whose enthusiasm for excellence in education made this book possible—I very appreciatively say: Thank you.

INTRODUCTION

I thought of how often as a writer I had made clear to myself some subject I had previously known nothing about just by putting one sentence after another—by reasoning my way in sequential steps to its meaning. I thought of how often the act of writing even the simplest document—a letter, for instance—had clarified my half-formed ideas. Writing and thinking and learning were the same process. (Zinsser, 1988, pp. viii-ix)

My father-in-law is one of those passionate gardeners for whom gardening is simultaneously an art and a science—a labor and a love. In late July, when all the lawns in St. Louis have turned to peanut brittle, Vasili is harvesting quarts of zucchini, tomatoes, bell peppers, carrots, eggplants, spinach, parsley, chamomile, basil, and chives from his terraced backyard oasis of scents and colors.

Vasili uses very few tools, but he does keep three shovels—each of them a different style. One afternoon, as I helped him restake the tomato plants, I asked him why he needed three kinds of shovels to maintain a garden of about 1,000 square feet. I expected a lengthy and reasoned comparison of handle lengths and leverage capabilities, blade shapes, and shoveling purposes. Instead, Vasili looked at me with his face screwed up in a grimace that indicated his amazement at my ignorance and said, "I have three shovels because different shovels do different things better."

Different Writing for Different Purposes

I tell you this story about my father-in-law's garden because it illustrates how different kinds of writing also serve different purposes. Just as Vasili found that shovels of various kinds were suited for specific gardening tasks (Yes, he did explain this later in the day during a dinner of fried eggplant, stuffed tomatoes, and sauteed sweet peppers and onions), so researchers have identified three different categories of writing activities—each of which serves a different purpose for students:

1. *Reflective or expressive writing* allows students to write about themselves and their reactions to new ideas and information. This kind of writing is often exploratory in nature; it can enable students to discover what it is they want to say or how they can best think through a problem.

2. *Informational or transactional writing* conveys verifiable information and tests previously learned knowledge. Most classroom writing activities are of this type.
3. *Poetic or imaginative writing* aims for an aesthetic or emotional response from the reader. (Martin et al., 1976; Applebee, 1984; Britton et al., 1975)

Classroom writing assignments are more often designed to show what students have already learned than to help with the learning process itself. (Applebee, 1984) This book does not focus on the kind of writing that tests what students should have learned, nor does it help you construct better essay exams or teach the five-paragraph theme more effectively (even though these topics are certainly worthy of consideration). Rather, our concern is with *personal* or *expressive* writing—the kind of writing that was mentioned first in the preceding list but that is seldom required in the classroom.

Reflective/Expressive Writing

This is the kind of writing that helps students more easily learn and retain what they have learned, that sharpens their critical thinking skills, and that deepens their appreciation for writing as a means of communication.

> Reflective/expressive writing utilizes each student's natural language and writing ability, regardless of any technical or grammatical shortcomings. It is writing that encourages students to raise questions and to "think on paper" without immediate concern for the mechanics of writing. It allows students to react to new ideas, to explore their own thoughts, to make mistakes (and correct them), and to work through problems.

These writing activities are not rigidly formatted, and the resulting papers are not treated as tests that require students to demonstrate knowledge or to give answers that are graded. Students are not evaluated on their ability to construct a formal essay and they are not graded for their skill in communicating ideas through writing. In effect, this kind of writing is similar to a discussion between two or more people, a conversation in which ideas are presented and alternatives explored. It is writing that allows students to find out what they already know or what they don't understand and want to find out.

The Organization of this Book

On the following pages you will see how to introduce your students to the benefits of writing in a variety of subjects including math, language arts, science, social studies, and art. It will also enable you to use these writing activities to cultivate your students' enthusiasm for learning, regardless of your subject area. Each chapter in this book includes an observation that allows you to enter a classroom and see how the teacher uses specific writing assignments to sustain and deepen students' interaction with subject matter:

Chapter One discusses **journal writing**, the popular and versatile activity that all students can use to help them begin writing to learn. In particular, we will look at two kinds of journal writing: individual journal entries and dialogue journals. These can help reinforce learning, build student confidence, and save time for the teacher.

Students in Carol Jenkins's mathematics classroom write **letters**, **radio broadcast scripts**, **personal narratives**, and **problem-solving explanations**. Chapter Two shows how *Writing Is Learning* helps Mrs. Jenkins' students develop their ability to think through and solve problems.

Mrs. Reeves uses **extended definitions**, **book reviews** (which are called **reading letters**), and **peer evaluations** to reinforce learning in her seventh- and eighth-grade language arts classes. Chapter Three discusses these activities and shows how teachers and other students respond to student writing.

The ability to **summarize** is important for all students. Chapter Four presents a variety of summary-writing activities that help students identify important information. **Essays** and **field notes from the future** are discussed along with other exercises in **note taking** and **letter writing**.

In Chapter Five our observation of Donald Vesta's language arts class shows how his eighth-grade students experience the relationship between writing and learning. Although letters have been mentioned in earlier sections of the book, this chapter focuses more extensively and specifically on **letter writing** as a way of learning. It also provides a good conclusion for the whole book as students describe the benefits they find in writing to learn.

In each chapter you will find these features:

- examples of student writing that resulted from using each activity in the classroom;
- detailed discussion showing how the writing exercises benefited students and teachers;
- writing prompts that teachers can use to spark useful and interesting responses from students; and
- strategies you can use to evaluate and comment on student writing.

Student writing examples included in this book are authentic and have not been edited for style, punctuation, grammar, spelling, or content. These samples should remind the reader that, when students write to learn, the emphasis is on learning and applying subject matter, not on writing skill. Finally, at the request of the school corporations whose staffs and students unselfishly cooperated in the development of this book, the actual names of persons and places have not been used.

One Student's Thoughts on Writing

This letter shows how one student felt about writing:

Dear Mr. Wills,

I use writing to help me study for different subjects in school. If I write something down I can see it, say it, hear it, and know it. Before I started doing this my test scores were not very good. Now that I write it down I can learn it better. Now my tests are improving and I am learning the subject materials better. I have found out the writing helps me alot. I use writing as an outlet to organize my thoughts.

Heather Van Dugen

You can see that Heather was well aware of a number of the benefits of using writing to learn. Similar letters will be included in Chapter Five, but for now Heather's comments will serve to remind us of the goal toward which we will be working throughout this book.

GETTING STARTED

Journals and Learning Logs

... the more that content is manipulated [by students],
the more likely it is to be remembered and understood.
In general, any kind of written response leads to better
performance than does reading without writing ...
(Langer and Applebee, 1987, p. 130)

Journals, also called reading logs or learning logs, are among the most popular and worthwhile types of reflective/expressive writing. All students can begin to keep journals even if they have not used other writing-to-learn activities in the past. *Journal entries* are very informal and can be used flexibly in all subjects to accomplish a variety of instructional goals. *Dialogue journals*, exchanged between students and teachers, use written conversation to personalize instruction and learning.

Keeping a Journal: A Personal Experience

Three years ago I was invited to teach technical report writing classes for undergraduate engineers. That position caused me to return to school for advanced degrees in education. When I resumed my university studies, after seventeen years in journalism and small business, I was surprised to learn that there was a new thing for graduate students to do: write in journals. We were told to carry a spiral notebook in which we could record our thoughts about what we were learning.

I was intrigued by the idea of commenting freely about my school work. In my previous years at school, teachers and professors had rarely asked me what I thought. They wanted to know, instead, what I had memorized.

I remember sitting in the library cafeteria one afternoon during my first week back at college. I had just finished the first reading assignment and opened my spiral-bound notebook, intending to record my thoughts about the reading. I casually wrote the date at the top of the first page. Below that, I scribbled the title of the chapter I had read. That's as far as I got. I didn't know how to begin keeping a journal.

I tell my technical writing students that occasionally I find writing to be terrifying. This has always intrigued me because there is no real danger in writing. I can rewrite or tear up anything I write. Nonetheless, writing sometimes gives me the sensation of climbing a high ladder and feeling a rung snap as I step on it.

That's the feeling of panic I had that day sitting in the basement of a library staring at a harmless sheet of paper. I didn't know what I wanted to say. I didn't know "what the professor wanted" me to say or how he wanted me to say it. I was afraid of the act of writing and of the consequences of my written words. Writing my reflections would expose what I didn't know. The prospect of writing about myself made me afraid of appearing vain. I was certain the professor would be put off by the peculiar way I use words and punctuation when I write informally. Years of journalism training and experience had not prepared me for this kind of writing. I was terrified.

Then I remembered the advice given by Robert Pirsig, a college writing instructor, to one of his rhetoric students in *Zen and the Art of Motorcycle Maintenance.* The student couldn't get started on a 500-word essay she wanted to write about the United States. Pirsig told her to narrow her topic and write about the town in which the college was located: Bozeman, Montana. She couldn't get started on that, either. Pirsig told her to narrow her topic to the main street of Bozeman. At the next class, in tears, the student told Pirsig that she still couldn't think of anything to write.

Pirsig, who refers to himself as "he" in this episode, describes what happened next:

> He told her angrily, "Narrow it down to the front of one building on the main street of Bozeman. The Opera House. Start with the upper left-hand brick."

> Her eyes, behind the thick-lensed glasses, opened wide.

She came in the next class with a puzzled look and handed him a five-thousand-word essay on the front of the Opera House on the main street of Bozeman, Montana. "I sat in the hamburger stand across the street," she said, "and started writing about the first brick, and the second brick, and then by the third brick it all started to come and I couldn't stop . . . (Pirsig, 1974, pp. 185-186)

I decided to pick one argument—one brick—in the chapter I had read and say what I thought about it. I started writing. My thoughts about the one argument grew into counter-arguments based on a few of my experiences. Writing about these experiences naturally brought others to mind, and I had to write about those, too. These experiences reminded me of reading I had done as a journalism major twenty years ago. I wrote about those readings, too. In doing this, I discovered how academic theories and focuses had changed in 20 years. I wrote about some of those changes, letting the spontaneous connections happen until I realized that I had written myself into agreement with the same arguments I had originally challenged.

I looked at my watch and was startled to see that I had written for 20 minutes about a topic to which I thought I had little response. The alchemy of writing had changed gripping fear into gripping questions that I wanted to ask the author, the professor, myself. I was already looking forward to the next class meeting—and the next reading assignment. Through journal-writing, my perception of myself as a student changed. I was more than a consumer and repeater of knowledge: I was a meaning-maker. I could see the connections between who I was, what I knew, and what I was learning.

Journal Entries

Journals, sometimes called reading logs or learning logs, are the most widely used of all writing activities. A journal is simply a personal diary in which students express their thoughts about their studies. They can use spiral-bound notebooks, loose-leaf binders, a separate file on a word processor—any convenient means for recording thoughts daily. Entries can be spontaneous or prompted or a combination, as the teacher directs.

Journals are popular with teachers because they can be used flexibly to reinforce a variety of instructional goals. Teachers can formulate writing prompts that encourage students to review, define, interpret, apply, and synthesize facts, concepts, and experience. Journal entries are easily and quickly skimmed periodically, and entries aren't graded for writing style. Additionally, journals can help teachers save time. As one English teacher told me:

> I'm amazed at how much I learn about student understanding, strengths and weaknesses, interests, learning styles, and general background knowledge when I read their responses. I've learned to *not* give instruction on matters that aren't relevant or needed. What I learn from student writing helps me examine priorities for classroom instruction.

Teachers find journals especially valuable because they are equally practical across all disciplines. They

---

are also popular with students because journal writing allows everyone to succeed. Students write in everyday language about themselves and their experiences and they can express opinions and feelings about what they are studying, which personalizes learning. Students can become risk-takers when they analyze and speculate about subject matter and use writing to think through a problem. Journal entries can provide students a personal record of learning that they can review for quizzes and exams.

Many teachers use journal writing to help students blend subject-area facts and concepts with their own outside knowledge and experiences. Here are two short journal entries, written by social studies students, that capture this blending of learning activities and students' prior knowledge, opinions, and experience.

Journal Entries

Student Writing Samples

I think the filmstrip started in the Holy land because first of all that's where the religions started. It also sort of showed how much the gov't was based on religion. We in the "west" take things much more for granted and most of us are not as religious.

Steven Ostrokol

> Mr. Frangello I would like to be in the Judaism group. I feel this because for one thing I *am* jewish. I also feel I have lots of resources available to me. Like my Hebrew School teacher. With my current knowledge I think I could make it an excellent project.
>
> Lisa Vogel

I have fun reading these journal entries. I like the way Steven and Lisa write confidently about who they are and what they know. I like their ability and willingness to blend their experiences with their school studies. Steven has some definite opinions about the way of life in the "west," which he applies to the content of the filmstrip. Lisa, as you can see, is already eager to do "field research" for her project. These writing samples show how journal writing can generate interest in a topic or a project. They also show how journal writing can add a special dimension to learning—validation—that other kinds of classroom activities might lack. Steven's and Lisa's journal entries also show how easy it is for students to succeed at journal writing; all they need is a pencil and a thought.

Teachers use journals in a variety of ways. Some use journal writing daily; others, weekly. Some teachers read students' entries; other teachers simply count entries to make certain that students are writing expected amounts. Some teachers grade journals for the quality of thinking reflected in entries; others don't grade journals at all. Carefully worded writing prompts are used by some teachers to excite students' prior knowledge or to help them recall, analyze, synthesize, or apply facts and concepts. Other teachers believe that unguided journal writing best supports learning because it encourages students to discover their own understandings. Many teachers use a blend of all of the above options according to students' needs, interests, and the subject matter at hand.

Unprompted Journal Writing

Reprinted below are several journal entries written by Masami Tanakasumo, a junior-high chemistry student. Her teacher encourages students to write journal entries at the beginning of each class. Masami's entries show that students focus on subject matter quickly and quietly when a class begins to keep journals. They also show that daily journal writing can bring continuity to learning as each day's activities become part of the next day's writing.

Journal Entry: Beginning of Class

Student Writing Sample

1-7-92 I wonder what chemicals are put together to make paper. Are the chemicals dangerous by themselves? Maybe it says on the package—I'll have to look next time.

1-8-92 I wonder what kind of lab we're doing today. I really do enjoy chemistry. It is not as hard as I thought it would be, it's easy and I actually understand it.

1-9-92 The lab I did yesterday was confusing. First of all, I did the lab wrong, and that means the questions are wrong. But we're going to do it over again.

1-10-92 I understand the lab that we did yesterday. It's basically the same idea as the others—neutralization. I wonder what lab we are doing today - if we are doing a lab.

I like the way Masami uses her journal to review, to anticipate, to summarize, and to ask questions. Her comment about the composition of paper brings up an important subject-related point that might have been lost if she had not written it down. When they read students' journals, some teachers look for these kinds of questions to spark lab activities or lesson plans that are especially meaningful to students.

Students can write in journals at any time during the class or the week. Many teachers give students much latitude regarding topics and content of journal entries. These teachers see journal writing as "sense-making" activities. As they "think on the page," students can develop fuller understandings of facts and concepts. Unprompted journal writing also lets students create their own connections between what they learn in class and what's happening in the real world. In particular, unprompted writing helps students discover for themselves what their interests are and how school studies reinforce those interests.

Here is a series of unprompted entries from middle-school student Aracelli Santos. You won't have any difficulty identifying Aracelli's interests and how she relates them to facts and concepts of her environmental science studies.

Unprompted Journal Entries

Student Writing Sample

2-4-92 We had a speaker today from Lake of the Woods. he was very interesting. I agree totally with his point of views. I think it's horrible that they are dumping that crap in the lake. The lake is really fun. It would be horrible if we had it no more.

2-6-92 I love sea otters. They have the cutest face. They are very playful. That's what I like in animals. I wish I could pet one.

2-10-92 I went to chicago this past week-end. It was a lot of fun. I saw beluga whales. They were so cute. They never stop smiling. It actually looked like they were talking to us. I wish I could go back.

2-26-92 There are so many animals that eat plankten. They will never become extinct because there is so many of them. I saw a video about them in Chicago. It was very interesting I advise you go to the oceanarium in Chicago. It tells you so much about all sealife.

You can see why students' journals are sometimes called *learning logs*. Students include important facts and concepts when they write about their experiences and their studies. This written record becomes a significant study aid at test time.

Here is series of entries from the journal of Crystal Stern, another environmentally aware junior-high-school student.

Unprompted Journal Entries

Student Writing Sample

11/27 I read the other day that the gray whale may be taken off the endangered lists. I'm glad that we are doing something to save the mammal, but I'm not so sure that it should be taken off the list. It won't receive as much protection and people may think that they need to stop worrying about whales, in general.

12/2 I bought alot of T-shirts and other items from those wildlife catalogs. Supposedly, the catalogs in turn make a contribution to preserving wildlife. so I guess I've made my contribution of the week.

12/5 I haven't heard anything about the environment lately, even in the paper. I have been looking for articles lately but I haven't seen anything. I woder if they've completely cleaned up the ocean near Kuwait. Ever since the war ended, we don't hear much about the clean-up.

I especially like Crystal's willingness to think through an issue and interpret facts beyond their surface meanings. I think Crystal shows sophisticated thinking in her concern that people might misinterpret the singular success of efforts to preserve the gray whale. I like the critical eye she casts toward news coverage of ocean cleanup efforts following Operation Desert Storm.

What would school be like for Crystal if her class didn't use journals to support classroom learning? Would Crystal be such an engaged learner—and critical thinker—if she didn't have a way to express her reflections? Would she care to ask the same kinds of questions about her studies and the real world? Without a journal, where would Crystal make sense and broaden her understandings through writing? Importantly, without the unique perspective offered by journal entries, Crystal's teacher might be denied a very special view of Crystal and how she understands her world. Journal entries like Crystal's make me wish journal writing was popular when I was her age.

Young Learners Write

Using a journal to learn and to reflect on ideas discussed in school can be effective at all ages. Some of the following notations may seem like comments an adult might make after reading a chapter on the solar system, but they come from nine- and ten-year-old students. The difference is that these children were jotting down the things that interested them; they were not studying for an exam. After reading a couple of chapters, James, nine years old, writes in his journal:

The solar system

A solar system is 2 or more planets orbiting a star. So a solar system is made up of a star and some planets and some moons. There are 9 planets in our solar system and they are Mercury, Venus, Earth, Mars, Jupiter, Saturn, Uranus, Pluto, and Neptune. They all orbit the sun and because the planets are diffrent sizes the months are longer or shorter than Earth.

At a nearby desk Carole was reading a book about astronomers. She became fascinated with Johannes Kepler and made the following comment in her journal:

There once was a boy named Johanas Kepler witch means John Kepler in German. John Kepler was a very smart kid. He got straight A's on his report card. Then one day a test on Astronomy. Then they took it. John finished first and his freind Billy came in second. Soon the results came out, he had gotten 100%. Soon John was a teenager. He took a ovnours class about astonomy and passed it. Soon John had to make a disision of the responce ubility about knowing what he wanted to be. It was 3 years before he knew what he wanted to be. He wanted to learn more about astomony. He was soon 35 years old when he first spotted Haley's Comet and he soon became famous.

Since Carole writes about the issues that she finds interesting, she and her teacher can focus on that instead of on the spelling and usage problems that appear in her writing. After all, the notes in a child's journal are for the benefit of the child; they are not for publication.

While James and Carole seem more interested in facts they have read in a science book, eleven-year-old Amy makes an editorial comparison between the human brain and computers:

Use Your Head

Most people really don't understand the human brain. It is the most perfectly designed and structured piece of material in the world. It has been this way for as long as humans have been living. Some people think, well wht about people that have disabilities. They have the capacity in there brain, but don't determine to learn anything.

Also people say, what about computers and state-of-the-art robots. They too are intelligent, but the human person built computers. So you see, some people are as smart and smarter than computers. New studies come up all the time about the brain. It is a magnificent creture.

Supporting Student Writing

As I discovered one afternoon in the university library cafeteria, keeping a journal can be hard, risk-taking work. Writer's block comes in many forms and can inhibit expression at even the most unlikely times. Some students might have difficulty thinking of a writing topic or adopting a conversational writing style.

Teachers can help students warm up to reflec-tive/expressive writing by keeping their own journals and by reading their journal entries to the class. Young writers who lack confidence can benefit from seeing the teacher write regularly and hearing how the teacher writes. It doesn't hurt young writers to see that adult writers sometimes chew on erasers instead of ideas, too.

Prompted Journal Writing

Teachers can use writing prompts to guide students' interaction with subject matter and provide a clearly defined writing topic. With prompted journal writing, teachers can direct students to the type of learning that best supports instructional goals. For instance, math teacher Walter Peach used a very specific prompt to focus his seventh-grade students' thinking and writing about graphs, as indicated by student Daniel O'Donnell's response printed below.

Prompted Journal Entry

Purpose: Define and apply.

Prompt: You are to write at least half a page (indent, use correct grammar) answering these questions:
>What are graphs?
>Where have you seen graphs?
>Who uses graphs?
>What are graphs for?
>Can you name any specific kinds of graphs?

Student Writing Sample

I have seen graphs in a lot of places. I mainly see them in the newspaper. They show how the stocks have gone up and down in the Business section. They're also used there to show the Economy falling from the years.

Graphs are used by alot of people. They are used by many scientists, and of course math teachers and students. I have used graphs alot in the past 3 years. We used them alot in social studies, and in science.

There are many kinds of graphs. I mainly use a bar graph, but there are line graphs, and pie graphs just to name a few. Line graphs are used to compare things from more than two years. Pie graphs are to show what percent of something you use like house expenses and clothes. Bar graphs are used to compare one subject in different times.

Daniel O'Donnell

Daniel certainly touched all the bases in his response: He was careful to answer each of Mr. Peach's questions about graphs. In doing so, Daniel produced a body of information about graphs that he can use later as a study aid. In a matter of seconds, Mr. Peach could skim this entry and get a good sense of Daniel's comprehension and accuracy. Or, this entry could be evaluated by other students in peer review sessions to reinforce classmates' knowledge and understanding of graphs.

Daniel's journal response, and the others you have read, contrast sharply with journal entries I read while visiting an eighth-grade English class last year.

Prompts for Young Learners

Some learners need more imaginative prompts to get them started in the direction in which the class discussion is headed. The two samples below came from social studies classes. In the first example, the teacher asked fourth-grade students to imagine that they were the principal of the school.

If I Ran a School

If I ran a school there would be no vilence and the kids would have to dress proper according to the rules, would not give there teacher a hard time or will be suspended and if there were vilence the vilent ones will be suspended for a day or two and I will have a teachers lunchroom, and a main office with five secretaries.

David

Wouldn't David's comments provide a stimulating kickoff for a discussion about the nature of rules in society or why safety in school and neighborhood is so important?

The next journal entry comes from an eighth-grade student who was encouraged to think about being president.

Will There Be a Women President?

Some people say that women are not able to be president of the united states. but that is not true just because they are the weaker sex dose not mean a thing

sometime women can do what men can do an even better so you can't tell me! that a lady cant be president and it just mite be a black one too! Before the year two thousand it is going to be a black man that's going to sit in the president's seat and it wont be long just wait you'll see!

By looking at student journals, social studies teachers can find issues that need to be discussed in our society. Even more significantly, they can find those issues coming from the thoughts of their own students.

Using the Short Story for Learning

Some teachers encourage students to express themselves by using the familiar short-story format to prompt students to write about a current topic or theme. One sixth-grade teacher, for example, had been discussing a typical food chain as part of a science lesson and then asked students to write a short story in their journals. "Perhaps," she said, "you could write about life before we had all the conveniences of freezers and food processing plants." Here's a story that grew out of her prompt:

Cavemen

Before the cavemen ate meat they ate bushes! Every single day they ate bushes. One day a caveman came in from a hard days work and said "Whats for dinner?" his wife said "bushes." he said "All my life Ive ate bushes time for something new" he thought for a minute and said "meat! Thats what I'll eat!" So he went out and saw 2 saber toothed tigers, so he picked up a stick and started sneaking up behind them. The one saber toothed tiger said to anouther "Don't look now but there's a cavemen with a stick walking up behind us. I think its the same one that got Barney yesturday." The other said thats terrible who's Barney" The other said "he's the one that lives on the hill, the one with one saber, and the lisp. "I think its the same one that hit me with a rock and run like hell." Lets get up and make alot of noise and maybe he'll run." So they got up and growled and snarled. But the cave-man stood still as a board, so they pounced on him, and let him lay. After that the caveman got up and staggered home. The next moring he made modern weapons for an easier kill. After that he went back to where he got tore up the other day, with his weapons. The 2 saber tooths were still there. He shot at one with a slinghsot but missed then they came after him, they cornered him! He said he will never hurt them again if they spare his life, so they did and he ran home and said "Time for more bushes."

Legitimate Concerns of English Teachers

Because they specialize in teaching writing skills, English teachers in particular may be uncomfortable with journals and other kinds of writing that permit a conversational style. English teachers may feel that all student writing must be letter perfect or marked down accordingly, and they may have more difficulty than social studies or math teachers in distinguishing between writing to learn and writing to show learning—distinguishing between the caliber of a student's *thinking* and the quality of the *finished writing product*.

These tensions are certainly understandable. We, too, favor high standards in language education and all subject areas. The issue, rather, hinges not on standards but on timing and instructional purpose. When students write to learn and to understand, *learning,* not writing skill, is the most important consideration. Additionally, English students' reflections recorded in journals often come to serve as the "first drafts" of more polished and structured work that is formally evaluated. As one teacher said, "I make sure the students review their journal entries for ideas before they start to write any particular kind of paper for a grade. Student's ideas usually work best for creative writing assignments. Principally, I use journal writing to help keep students thinking and interested in writing and learning."

Dialogue Journals

Dialogue journals let teachers and students talk to each other through writing. Using spiral notebooks or electronic mail, students write expressively about what they are learning and about their learning processes. In their journals, students can speculate, ask questions, or express opinions. Periodically these notebooks are given to the teacher, who reads the students' thoughts, responds constructively in writing, and returns the books to the students for the next exchange.

Dialogue journals provide students with personalized encouragement and feedback, and they provide teachers with insights regarding what students are learning and how students are applying their knowledge. Teachers use these journals for a variety of instructional purposes: to activate prior knowledge, keep track of and direct learning in progress, and reinforce instruction. Exchanging dialogue journals sounds like more work than it is. These journals aren't graded; teachers can skim them for key words.

Teacher's responses can be short and to the point. In *The Journal Book,* Toby Fulwiler talks about Leslee Reed, a sixth-grade teacher who pioneered the use of dialogue journals in the 60's. Fulwiler explains how dialogue journals helped Reed teach more effectively and efficiently:

> She quickly found that the time she spent in responding (about an hour for sixth grade; less for primary students) was not only enjoyable, but that in the same hour she could do most of her lesson planning for the next day. This daily written feedback also led to the elimination of many busy-work assignments which didn't have much meaning for the students or her. (Fulwiler, 1987, p. 51)

However, there's no rule that says journals need to be exchanged daily or that teachers have to respond to every entry.

Dialogue writing is fun. I look forward to conversing in writing with engineering students in my technical report writing classes. The process is simple: They write something to me about content or class activities and I respond with praise for their insights and suggest questions that they might think about. These exchanges aren't evaluated and don't affect students' grades. I don't correct their grammar, even though ours is a writing class. I prefer to exchange sheets of paper, not spiral notebooks. I write my part of the conversation on their sheets and give them back. Students keep these chronologically ordered in their class notebooks.

Coaching instead of Teaching

Dialogue writing helps me learn things about my students that can help me instruct more efficiently and effectively. I can provide students with timely and friendly feedback that can save instructional hours. Dialogue writing lets me coach instead of teach. These written conversations let students practice thinking on the page about technical writing and the specific problems they're writing about. This kind of writing practice builds students' confidence in their writing because papers aren't criticized for vocabulary or grammar.

Some students respond fluently when asked to write expressively for a dialogue journal. Many students do not. To help my students focus their writing, I ask them to answer specific questions that are directly related to instructional input and their learning. I try not to have students write—even expressively—just to practice writing.

I use dialogue journals as a kind of prewriting exercise to help students focus on the technical problem they're dealing with and how they plan to write about it. Here's an example in which Parsa Patel "described" a report she was beginning to write.

Dialogue Journal: Beginning of Unit
Student Response/Teacher Response

Prompt: Describe the report you are planning to write.

Parsa responds:

1. Comparisons of facts of where we have been & where we stand at this time.

2. Ideas on where the problems lie & what we can do about it.

3. Some results & possibilities, now that there is more focus on improving the situation.

This entry told me that Parsa was thinking not only about the topic problem but also about its history and context: she had the right approach. Her three areas of focus were likely to give the report much of its structure: her thinking was organized. I could see, however, that she hadn't yet focused on her problem at an evidenciary level: She had no information to write about.

I wanted to tell Parsa to get some facts to fit into the framework of her inquiry. I wanted to suggest what types of information she needed and where to look for it. I wanted to say these things in a few friendly comments that wouldn't sound like criticism. I also wanted to acknowledge and encourage her organized thinking.

I respond: Details say more than generalities. I've circled several areas you've identified where specific information can really tell your story. Good job of picking out the skeleton.

Comments such as this are not peculiar to teaching students how to write technical reports. Teachers of all subjects make these kinds of comments daily in speech and writing to direct and encourage student learning. Parsa told me later that this particular dialogue helped her save hours of writing and thinking when she began her first drafts. I saved time, too, when she produced a final report that needed fewer comments and corrections.

I also use dialogue journal exchanges at the end of a study unit to discover what students learned and to reinforce that learning. Each semester, students write a procedure manual. First drafts are revised according to suggestions made in peer-review sessions. I read the second drafts and comment freely, but I don't give the manuals a grade. Instead, students have to think through my suggestions as they incorporate or challenge my suggestions for the final draft. This second rewriting prevents students from forgetting my comments after they have read them. These final drafts are also circulated in class and reviewed, so students can learn by comparison. It's twice the work for everyone, but the benefits justify the time and effort. Students gain confidence as writers and gain skill as editors and collaborative learners, as their comments below indicate. After the third drafts are graded and returned, I engage in a dialogue with my students to discover and reinforce what they learned about manuals and the process of writing them.

Dialogue Journal: End of Unit Student Response/Teacher Response

Prompt: Review the first, second, and third drafts of your manual. How are they different? What did you learn about manuals and about writing manuals?

Brett responds: I learned that there are many different ways to prepare a manual. In these manuals, it is easier to understand the process when the steps are numbered and a brief explanation follows rather than writing the instructions out in a paragraph form. It is much easier to understand directions when they are brief & specific instead of wordy & vague. (I also learned that not everyone would enjoy changing the oil in a VW).

I respond: These are very important things to learn. Good observations. I hope you had fun learning these things. Importantly, *writing* a manual is also easier when lists are employed. Figures help, too.

Theresa responds: I learned that the guidelines of using lists, white space, indentations, etc. really do help in reading a manual. Also, I learned that simple and economical use of language also facilitates reading a manual. You don't get so bogged down trying to follow the directions when they are straight and to the point. Illustrations also help quite a bit in aiding the reader in understanding the manual.

I respond: This represents an excellent summary of some the considerations that are critical to effective technical writing in general and manuals in particular.

Responses in dialogue journals can be short and to the point. Teachers need write only enough to validate and reinforce learning.

These exchanges with my students told me what kind of learning was happening in class. Responses verified that students had come to value lists, logical organization, attractive layout, graphics, and clear and concise instructions as important elements of a "reader-friendly" procedure manual. I hope that my responses to the students validated and reinforced their learning. Importantly, these written conversations required less time than actual conversations would have required.

Dialogue journals can be exchanged at any time to provide students with opportunities to review their learning, ask the teacher questions, express their opinions and understandings, and make meaningful interpretations about their learning. These exchanges, whether daily, weekly, or monthly, help teachers learn what students are learning. Teachers can use these written conversations to coach and encourage students.

Sharing Thoughts about Books

Parents and teachers might use the dialogue-journal concept as a way of conversing with children about the books they have read in common. In fact, the journal may be an efficient way to reflect on and exchange ideas about the books that any two or more people have read. Fiction as well as nonfiction can be used for this purpose. Whether the dialogue involves two children or a child and an adult, the mechanism serves to encourage thought, praise, questions, or requests for clarification.

Here's what Becky, a seventh-grader, said about the dialogue she and her mother have about books they are reading in common:

> We usually read on our own and then talk about the book. We have a dialogue journal and I always write to my mom in it. I'm always asking her, "How are you doing?" This has been fun to do.

I suppose that children are intrigued by the opinions their parents, teachers, or friends may express about these shared experiences. As the dialogue grows, of course, each participant can raise questions and give his or her own interpretation. The dialogue starts with one statement prompted by whatever is happening in the book. Here, for example, is the start of a dialogue journal concerning the book *The City of Gold and Lead:*

> When the world was new, people were fighting. Right now people are fighting. People will always be fighting. Why do people fight? I wish there could be world peace. Why are there wars? The world is in turmoil and who cares about my small problems? Who cares about a town of 10,000 people in Wyoming? (Michael)

Response: I care, and so do a lot of other people. The world is made up of small towns. More people care about small towns than care about big cities. Besides, the beginning of this book also shows you that the two boys are trying to do something that will make their lives better—away from war. Let's keep thinking about how we can make our lives better even though there are wars going on all over the place. What do you think we could do right here in Wyoming?

Using These Activities in Your Classroom

This chapter gives examples of how teachers use journal writing

- to start thinking about a theme or topic,
- to aid the study of particular topics,
- to prompt interest and discovery, and
- to engage in dialogue to coach and encourage students.

Why Journals?

Journal writing is easy to start (just get a notebook) and does not carry any threat of evaluation. It is a tool for thinking and learning, not a place where kids can get skewered.

How Can I Get Started?

Just do it! All the student needs is a notebook or a folder that will hold daily notes. But in order for the activity to serve their learning, you need to focus on it. Journal writing needs to become routine: every day, or at least every other day. Keep the writing period short—about five to eight minutes, depending on the age of the student. Then, from time to time, ask for volunteers to read their thoughts on particular topics or events.

How Can I Keep It Interesting?

Even though journal writing may often be personal, it helps for the teacher to select passages to read aloud or to have the writer read aloud. Naturally, any passage that is labeled private or personal is off limits.

Some teachers ask students to fold in half any page that they do not want anyone to read. On the other hand, there will be many times when students want the teacher to respond to a particular page or section. These sections can be marked with a colored pencil as a signal for the teacher to pay particular attention.

Sometimes it helps to give students class points for participating actively in journal writing. One teacher I know gives points for journal entries that are at least a hundred words long. Shorter entries are not counted. He claims that both quality and quantity of entries improved by using that simple technique with his high-school freshmen.

The most effective way to make journal writing interesting is to get other people involved in reading or responding to what the students have written. Whether their peers, family members, or the teacher, the fact that someone else will read some of the entries and talk about what has been written will often stimulate learning effectively through journal writing. Some teachers actually distribute sheets of paper that display a wide column for the original journal entry and a narrow column for the comments of readers.

How Can I Evaluate Journal Writing?

Even though journals are not meant to be evaluated for English proficiency or subject matter, there are two kinds of subtle evaluation that promote better journal writing. One is the simple requirement of minimum length for one day. The other is raising questions for clarification. Whether the teacher or a peer reads an entry, each should feel free to identify statements that are not clear. When a reader says that something is difficult to understand, the writer begins to realize that more needs to be said or that thoughts need to be expressed more clearly. Gradually, these requests for clarity will have the desired effect: more precise learning and clearer communication.

PUTTING IDEAS IN ORDER

Narratives and Problem Solving

Every opportunity for the students to talk on the page
about what they're learning reinforces their learning.
(Carol Jenkins, teacher)

Narratives, letter writing, role playing, and two
types of problem-solving explanations reinforce
learning in Carol Jenkins' seventh- and
eighth-grade mathematics classes. We suggest
prompts that make these activities practical in
other subject areas.

The walls of Carol Jenkins' eighth-grade math
class are covered with posters, equations, newspaper
and magazine clippings. Cartoons, comic strips, and
students' writings about math embellish the bulletin
boards.

Mrs. Jenkins explains her room's decor by saying, "The students bring things in and ask if they can display them. They're constantly looking for things outside school that show that mathematics is something we use every day. They understand that math is not just something we learn about in school."

I asked, "How do your students feel about writing about math?"

"At first the students expressed some resistance to all this writing about math," she said. "But now they don't even think of writing as separate from math. They think that writing *is* problem solving."

Mrs. Jenkins explained that she uses a variety of writing activities for students to explain and use math concepts and skills. "Every opportunity for students to talk on the page about what they are learning reinforces their learning," she said.

Narratives: Real-World Applications

"At the beginning of the fall semester, I'll ask them to describe how they used math over the summer vacation," she explained. "I ask them to be specific, to name the specific math skills they used. I'm looking for more than a story about how they counted money. You'd be surprised at some of the incidents the students report, especially the eighth-grade students. I've had students write that they used math to help their parents with income and sales taxes and figuring percentages. My overall goal," Mrs. Jenkins said, handing me a sheet of paper from a folder on her desk, "is to get the students to connect math with daily life, as Courtney Evans did in this paper."

Narrative: Real-World Applications— Summer Vacation

Purpose: To remind students of their prior knowledge of the subject or topic, allow them to review knowledge, and help them discover real-life importance of facts, concepts, and skills.

Prompt: Math is used in the "real world" every day. Give some examples of how you used math this summer. What specific skills were used?

Evaluation: Check for understanding.

Student Writing Sample

Math in the Real World

This summer I used math in many ways. I am on the ABC swim and dive team. When I am swimming in a event at a swim meet, I like to know what my average time is. To find this I have to use addition and division. Say in my last three meets, I had gotten three times in an event:

0:36, 0:38, 0:34

I would average these times together by adding them:

0:36 + 0:38 + 0:34 = 1 min. 48 sec.

Now that I have my sum I would divide it by three, because there are three figures in the sum. If there were four figures I would divide it by four.

1 min. 48 sec. ÷ 3 = 108 sec. ÷ 3 = 36 sec.

Following these steps I have found my average time: 36 sec.

. . . I also mowed lawns and babysat. I used addition, subtraction, division, and multiplication. I needed knowledge of those technical skills to manage my money.

I used math all summer and although I don't always enjoy math class - without math I might not have had as much fun last summer!

Courtney Evans

In this paper, Courtney not only described how she used "Math in the Real World" during the summer break but also associated math skills with her summer fun and swimming successes! Such pleasurable associations can help keep students interested in any school subject.

Here's how another student used "Math in the Real World" during the summer vacation.

Narrative: Real-World Applications— Summer Vacation

Student Writing Sample

I used mental math when I went shopping. When I bought more than one thing I would add up the price tags to see how much it would cost. Also, when something was on sale I would figure out how much I got off by using multiplication, subtraction, and addition. An example would be when a sweater was $49.99 and on sale for 25% off. I would first round up to $50.00. Then I would take off 10% which is $5.00, another 10% which is also $5.00, and then 5% which is one-half of 10% to get $2.50. Then I would add all those together, my sum being $12.50, and subtract my total from the price. So the price would be $37.50.

I went to Georgia over the summer to visit a friend. I had to pay for the plane ticket and other things. I had to manage and earn my money so I wouldn't run out.

Becky Montgomery

It sounds like Becky also had fun using math during her summer vacation. She certainly understands that percentages aren't something that students study in school just to pass tests. I like her "shorthand" way of figuring percentages. It's the same one I use. And I like the way she remembered to say that she rounded up $49.99 to $50.00. It shows that she's aware of her thinking processes when she averages numbers.

"Real World Applications" help Mrs. Jenkins' students focus on how they actually used math skills over the summer vacation. For this reason, Mrs. Jenkins explained, it's an especially effective way to generate student interest in math at the beginning of the fall semester. The writing activity also helps to activate students' prior knowledge of math in those critical first few days back at school.

Teachers in any content area can use exercises similar to the "Real World Applications—Summer Vacation" example. Here are a few other prompts for narratives in other subjects:

- How Did I Use Geography This Summer?
- How Did My Reading Skills Help Me Have Fun This Summer?
- What Questions About Biology Did I Discover This Summer?

Because these narratives ask students to review subject-area knowledge and skills and apply them to real-life situations, they can be used at any point in the semester. Prompts such as "How Do I Exercise My Bill of Rights Freedoms" or "How Many Birds Can I Name and How Do I Tell Them Apart?" are mid-semester writing topics that can reinforce skills and information learned in a particular unit.

Importantly, "Real World Application" narratives aren't limited to first-person stories. Hypothetical situations can also be used to prompt "Real World" stories that help students review and apply facts and concepts. "What would happen if...?" stories can be used in any subject area to help students review and apply what they know and how it relates to real life. "What would happen to our food supply if plants didn't have carbon dioxide?" or "What would happen if we didn't have relative pronouns?" are writing prompts about hypothetical situations that can cause students to think about and appreciate school studies. Student narratives can provide teachers with useful insights into what students have learned and how they apply new skills and information.

Peer Dialogues: Letters

Because of the variety of approaches, reflective/expressive writing brings flexibility to teaching. Writing can build upon other related activities or can go in new directions that reflect changing student interests or instructional goals.

"We started with the students writing letters to each other about what was happening in class," Mrs. Jenkins explained. "Then we expanded their reading audience to include the students in the sixth-grade class, to see if they could explain math concepts to a younger audience. Of course, the sixth-grade students benefit, too. They gain exposure to some of the concepts they will encounter in eighth grade," Mrs. Jenkins said, as she produced another student paper from her folder.

Peer Dialogues: Letters

Purpose: To help students review, explain, and apply facts, concepts, and skills.

Prompt: Write a letter to a sixth-grade friend explaining the order of operations. Tell the importance of doing things in order. Include examples.

Evaluation: Check for accuracy and understanding.

Student Writing Sample

Dear Kristin,

So how is Ms. Delaney's sixth grade math? Are you learning a lot these days? In our math class we were told to write a letter to a sixth grader explaining the order of operations. This is really important to learn and memorize. You don't just use order of operations in math either. In the real world you wouldn't put your shoes on before your socks or you wouldn't brush your teeth before putting on the toothpaste. It's a little more complicated in math. You must memorize the following. "Please Excuse My Dear Aunt Sally." If you can remember that saying you are on your way to success!

The word *please* stands for parentheses. That's the first thing you would do. That is anything inside parentheses.

The word *excuse* is for exponents. Any exponents in a problem you would do second.

The two words *my dear* go together. The *my* is for multiplication and the *dear* is for division. If a problem has both you would do whichever comes first.

Last is *Aunt Sally* which stands for *addition* and *subtraction*. Both of these are also whichever comes first in the problem.

Here is an example. It's going to seem pretty complicated but you must remember to be patient.

6^2	+	5 −	13(6+4x5)	1st parentheses
6^2	+	5 −	13(6+20)	2nd parentheses
6^2	+	5 −	13(26)	3rd exponents
36	+	5 −	13(26)	4th multiplication
36	+	5 −	388	5th addition
41	−	388		6th subtraction
297				7th answer

> Step by step it was pretty easy. You just have to take your time. Remember the saying, "Please Excuse My Dear Aunt Sally." Which stands for:
>
> Please - Parentheses
> Excuse - Exponents
> My - Multiplication
> Dear - Division
> Aunt - Addition
> Sally - Subtraction
>
> Your friend, Shana

Shana seems to relish the opportunity to show off her math skills to a younger student. Young adolescents especially like to talk about themselves to their friends and peers. When they can't talk, they write notes to each other. Peer dialogues can be written as letters, notes, or any form that combines subject learning with students' natural desire to communicate with their friends.

Letters to Aliens

The informal nature of reflective/expressive writing allows Mrs. Jenkins to capitalize on students' emerging interests as she reinforces math learning. Letter writing provides a good way for students to write freely and imaginatively about math, especially when the letters can be sent to anyone in the solar system.

"We let the students write letters to aliens on other planets to see if the students could explain how numbers are used, and their importance, on earth. The students try to explain to the aliens how numbers could be useful to them on their own planets," Mrs. Jenkins said, handing me another sheet of paper. "The actual prompt for this activity was 'Write a letter to an alien visiting our planet.' In your letter explain the concept of signed numbers. The alien has never seen numbers preceded by a + or –. But any similar prompt about any math topic would work just as well," she said.

Letters to Aliens

Purpose: To help students review, explain, and apply facts, concepts, and skills.

Prompt: Write a letter to an alien visiting our planet. In your letter explain the concept of "signed numbers." The alien has never seen numbers preceded by a + or –.

Evaluation: Check for understanding and accuracy.

Student Writing Sample

Dear alien from another planet,

Here on Earth we have many different types of numbers. Today I am going to explain positive and negative integers. Integers are numbers.

A positive number is any number that is to the right of zero on a number line. The numbers 1, 2, 3, and 4 are some examples of positive numbers. There are many, many more.

A negative number is a little more complicated. A negative numbers is any number to the left of zero on a number line. In other words the value of a negative number is less than zero. If you add a positive number and a negative number together it's the same as subtracting the negative number from the positive number. For example, 2 + -1 is the same as 2 – 1.

Sincerely,
Tony Carli

This letter, from Earth student Tony Carli to a visiting space alien, continued for another page. I've reprinted enough of Tony's letter to show how writing letters, even to an alien, can help students recall, understand, and apply their new facts and concepts.

Teachers in any subject area can use "Letters to Aliens" to enhance students' recall, understanding, and application of facts, concepts, and skills. Some effective prompts might be these:

- Describe Harmony to an Alien.
- Describe Cell Division to an Alien.
- Explain the Concept of One Person/One Vote to an Alien.

While writing these letters, students can discover information they haven't yet learned or don't fully understand. Students might need to review material as they write their letters. That's OK. These writing activities are meant to promote learning; they are not examinations.

Role Playing

Mrs. Jenkins took another student writing sample from her folder. "Sometimes we use the format of a radio reporter," she said. "Parts per million is a difficult concept for eighth-graders to grasp. In our writing about the concept, we adopted the approach of a reporter broadcasting live from Fenger Middle School as water was added to dilute a solution of 20,000 parts per million and the solution was repeatedly tested for it concentration. As you can see," Mrs. Jenkins said, "some students can get very creative in writing about math."

Role Playing: Scriptwriting—Radio Reporter

Purpose: Students demonstrate understanding of processes or concepts by describing related chains of events.

Prompt: Explain how manipulatives helped your understanding of parts per million. Explain the concept of parts per million.

Evaluation: Check for understanding and accuracy.

Student Writing Sample

Hi! This is Kara Zdanowski reporting live from the paper strip at Fenger Middle School. I have just transformed myself into a green dye section on one part of the strip of ten sections. So, I am only one out of ten sections. We can call the other sections water. But wait! Help! There are more water strips coming in on top of me! Umph! There, ha! I pushed them aside. Wait a minute. I counted 9 more strips come in on me. But if there are 9 more strips with 10 sections each, I am only 1 in 100 or 1/100. Ah! So much water, so little me! I can't stand it! Oh no. Not again. More water. I am going to disappear very soon! Now I counted 1000 sections! Ahhh! Now I am only 1/1000. Bmphfh! I'm getting suffocated by sections of water. Ahh! This is probably going till 1,000,000 sections of water. Oh no. I had to open my big mouth. Well, so long world, so long earth, so long everyone! I am going to become so faint, you won't be able to see me! I am 1 part per million or 1/1,000,000. All this for a stupid job with no break. Well so long and I hope my risking my life has helped you understand parts per million. Bye, ahh!

Scriptwriting helped Kara discover a creative way to explain, apply, and remember the important concept of parts per million. Her explanation is one that I, too, will certainly remember for a long time.

Scriptwriting is easy to use in any subject area to encourage students to recall and review knowledge. As with letters, scriptwriting capitalizes on students' natural desire to communicate to their friends. Gregarious students might enjoy reading their radio scripts to the class; this can be entertaining as well as educational. As students read their news reports, the other students gain additional exposure to your subject matter. Such an activity gives your teaching variety, which can be important in a class of students with varied learning styles.

Scriptwriting is not limited to the role of radio news reporter. Students can be asked to imitate radio and television commercial scriptwriters. Literature students could be asked to write a television or radio commercial "previewing" a book or story they are reading. How would a broadcast ad-person hook an audience for Macbeth? What descriptors could be used? What action in the play could be described? By asking students to write a commercial for Macbeth or any other piece of literature, English teachers encourage students to reflect on the characters, events, and themes of the work.

Real-Life Roles

Real-life controversies and issues can provide students a variety of roles for letter writing. In the following writing sample from a social studies class, Julie Bartholomew pretends she is an executive writing a letter to an editor about an important environmental issue: toxic waste incineration. This writing assignment was part of a learning unit focusing on environmental issues and the political process. In this unit, students researched and presented multiple perspectives surrounding the disposal of buried toxic wastes discovered in the fictional town of Jonesville.

Role Playing: Chemical Company Executive

Purpose: To help students develop critical thinking skills and multiple perspectives when they review, interpret, summarize, and apply facts and concepts to formulate and defend opinions about an issue.

Prompt: As the executive of the chemical company, write a letter to the editor of the *Jonesville Tribune.* State your choice for the cleanup. Give the advantages and disadvantages for this method. Support your choice with evidence given at the town meeting. Use correct letter-writing procedure.

Student Writing Sample

November 17, 1992

Dear Editor,

I am the vice-president of the XYZ Agricultural Chemical Company and I would like to give you my opinion about what solution I think would be best to clean up the contaminated areas. I feel that excavation and incineration would be the best way. It's not very expensive and its very reliable and there are no harmful long term effects. Since the molecules in the pesticide will be broken down during the process they will be harmless when they are let out into the air. I hope to see my opinion published in the paper soon.

Sincerely, Julie Bartholomew

Julie presented a persuasive case for incineration of harmful pesticides currently buried somewhere in Jonesville. She builds her case on cost and safety. Other students in her class wrote letters to the editor from different roles that individuals would play in a similar real-life controversy. In the following letter, student Bill Black writes from the role of a concerned citizen.

Role Playing: Concerned Citizen

Purpose: To help students develop critical thinking skills and multiple perspectives when they review, interpret, summarize, and apply facts and concepts to formulate and defend opinions about an issue.

Prompt: As a concerned citizen, write a letter to the editor of the *Jonesville Tribune*. State your choice for the cleanup. Give the advantages and disadvantages for this method. Support your choice with evidence given at the town meeting. Use correct letter-writing procedures.

Student Writing Sample

Dear Editor,

After hearing about 4 companies procedures at the town meeting, I have come to a conclusion that containment is the answer. Mr. Smith and Mr. Adams explained their plan. They want to use clay. A disadvantage would be the clay adventually cracking and leaking. They promise to replace the clay at no cost if this happens. They have tested their plan before and almost guarantee it. Even though the cost is $300,000 dollars, which is not the most expensive, it seems to be the most logical one. XYZ Chemical had no idea what they were doing . . .

Sincerely,
Bill Black

Bill Black's letter to the editor continues for another page. I've reprinted enough of it to demonstrate how role playing encourages students to review and think critically about subject-area facts, often from a new perspective and toward new conclusions. Interestingly, both Bill and Julie cited the advantages of cost and safety in their arguments supporting different disposal methods. I wonder what students would say in class discussion about Julie's and Bill's conflicting use of the same information?

Teachers in any discipline can find contemporary controversies and issues to spark similar role playing that focuses and reinforces learning in content areas. Science teachers can have students research and discuss from multiple perspectives the merits of expensive space shuttle operations or the proposed orbiting space station. Social studies teachers can build writing projects around political processes affecting school choice, state-chartered gambling operations, and the homeless. Economics teachers can use such activities to present and examine the economic impact of increased fuel taxes, trade restrictions, or changes in social security legislation.

Writing about Problem Solving

Mrs. Jenkins uses a highly structured writing format when students describe their mathematics problem-solving processes. "I have the students write a paragraph describing their understanding of the problem. They write a paragraph describing strategies they use to solve the problem. Then they write a paragraph about the solution and how they know it's the right answer. This paragraph is the difficult one for them to write. How do they know the number three is the right answer? Then they write a paragraph about their reflections. Can they make up a new problem that can be solved with a similar process? Or perhaps they talked to a friend and learned a better or easier way to solve the problem."

She handed me the following sample, written by Robert Ward, so that I could see how the format works. I've reprinted all of Robert's lengthy explanation so that you can see how each section conforms to Mrs. Jenkins' format.

Problem Solving: Structured Explanation

Purpose: To help students develop critical thinking skills when they review and describe their problem-solving procedures and apply new skills, facts, or concepts to real life.

Prompt: Measure the density of marshmallows when the volume is changed but the mass remains constant. Use a balance scale and graduated cylinder to complete this.

Evaluation: Check for understanding and accuracy.

Student Writing Sample

Understanding: The compaction lab is used all the time in the real world. I think of compaction going on in a landfill. Some houses use garbage compactors to conserve the space for garbage at home. Compaction is done so less space is used. This lab will help me understand the importance of compaction for everyday life.

Strategy: The best way to go about any lab is to follow directions. I used a chart to keep track of all the information I had collected. The chart showed the mass, volume, and density for before and after compaction with the marshmallows. With a chart it was much easier to compare the before and after results.

In the directions, they said to measure the mass of the cylinder alone. the cylinder weighed 13.9 grams. Then I had to gently put 20 marshmallows in the cylinder and weigh them on the scale. The marshmallows and the cylinder weighed a total of 24.4 grams. The next directions told me to find the mass of just the marshmallows.

$24.4 - 13.9 = 10.5$ grams (the mass of just the marshmallows before compaction)

After figuring the mass of just the marsh-mallows, I recorded the data on my chart. The next step told me to find the volume of the marshmallows before compaction. That was very easy. All I had to do was look off the side of graduated cylinder. The marshmal-lows with all the air between them went up pretty high, 70 milliliters. The next step was to find the volume. More math was involved in this step. I had to divide mass by volume.

10.50 gm. ÷ 70 ml. = .15g/ml.

Since I was dividing grams by milli-liters, you had to represent that by writing grams/milliliters.

The next step was to compact the marshmallows to as little space as pos-sible. After compacting the marshmallows to as small as I could, I had to record the mass, volume, and density all over again. I did this to see if compaction really does make a difference in mass, volume, and density. I again weighed the graduated cylinder on the balance containing the compacted marshmallows. There was a little difference in mass. It seemed that the weight had become less. It was only 10.1 grams instead of 10.5 grams. (The volume was clearly going to be different after compaction). The volume read on the side of the cylinder was 30 ml. It had made a great difference in space by compacting the marshmallows. To find the density I divided mass by volume,

10.1 gm. ÷ 30 ml. = .336 g/ml.

Marshmallow Lab Chart

Before Compaction

Mass	Volume	Density
10.5 gm.	70 ml.	.15 g/ml.

After Compaction

Mass	Volume	Density
10.1 gm.	30 ml.	.336 g/ml.

Reflections: Before compaction there was a lot of space taken up by air between the marshmallows. They were very light and fluffy. Although marshamllows weigh very little in the first place, they can still weigh less after compaction. The marshmallows were forced to be in a tiny space so they had to get closer together. Compaction is very important in landfills. We could save so much space by compacting. Even though not all items can be compacted to as small as the marshmallows, but every little bit helps on taking up less space.

Robert W. Ward

Problem solving isn't easy and neither is writing about it, but both activities have important benefits for students and teachers. Had Robert erred in his technique or his calculations, he might have discovered the error while writing about his experience. In reliving the compaction experiment as he wrote, Robert gained reinforcement of skills and concepts needed to perform the experiment. This also increased Robert's time on task—a critical aspect of learning.

From students' problem-solving papers, teachers can learn what processes students followed or which steps students skipped or completed incorrectly. Teachers can also learn how students integrate their learning with their knowledge of the everyday world.

Mrs. Jenkins' format for this type of writing is worth noting. The format requires students first to formulate and express their understanding of the assigned problem. Students then describe their problem-solving process and must defend their answer. Finally, students have to apply their learning to a real-life situation. These ways of looking at problem solving in any subject area help students develop and direct critical thinking skills.

Teachers in other subject areas can use problem solving to reinforce specific skills or subject matter and foster students' skills in thinking critically. Mrs. Jenkins' format can be employed as presented or adapted by teachers in any subject area to suit a class of students, a topic, or a specific problem. An American history prompt might be "How did the founding fathers solve the problem of state interference with religious practices? How do we know their solution worked?" A life science problem might be "Devise an experiment that demonstrates that carbon monoxide gas is poisonous. How do you know the experiment will work?" Writing such as this asks students to identify, analyze, synthesize, and apply information that you know is important for them to learn and understand.

Problem solving that is less formally structured may be more suitable for certain types of problems, according to Mrs. Jenkins. Students can simply explain the solutions they've discovered; they don't always have to apply them to real-life situations.

Problem Solving: Simple Explanation

Purpose: To help students use their subject knowledge to discover multiple solutions to a problem.

Prompt: If a circle has no center shown, how many ways can you find the center?

Evaluation: Check for understanding and accuracy.

Student Writing Sample

I could fold a paper circle into 4 equal parts. Where the 2 fold lines intersect, that would be the center.

I could punch 3 holes on the edge of a paper circle, attach strings and find the center of gravity, which would be the center.

I could draw three lines across the diameter in different spots, the intersection would make the point.

I could measure the diameter, then make a compass half the diameter, then draw arcs from the edge of the circle.

Eilene Gottschalk

I especially like Eilene's writing sample because it illustrates Mrs. Jenkins' comment that students occasionally give the right answer without fully understanding the subject matter or its application. Eilene might be able to answer a multiple-choice test question correctly about the midpoint of the diameter of circle indicating the circle's center. However, Eilene's problem-solving explanation shows that she hasn't quite learned to apply that information effectively.

This kind of feedback is important to a teacher. The other solutions which Eilene explains indicate that she does have a good grasp of alternative ways to determine the center of a paper circle.

At this point in our conversation, I told Mrs. Jenkins that, like her students, I was also convinced that writing *is* math problem solving. I said I understood the many ways her math students benefited when they wrote about what they were studying. I wanted to know, however, how reflective/expressive writing helped her teach more easily and effectively. Didn't these activities create more work for her?

Less Time Reteaching

"For one thing," she explained, "I get to learn more specifically about what each child knows. I get to see more than just their numbers on a page. Getting the right answer in math doesn't always mean the student understands the process. Students can get good at playing the game of finding the pattern and picking the 'right' numbers for answers."

"I also find I spend less time at the front of the class. I spend more time with students and answering their questions. I think I probably spend less time reteaching, too," she said.

Kathy Adams, a seventh-grade science teacher, gave this report:

Depending on the type of writing, a variety of information can be gained. Sometimes you may find out where you need to begin new learning. Other times you find out what interests the students. Information from students can often lead me to adjust my instruction to fit their needs or interests. If you find out that the students already know something you had planned on covering, you can go on to the next level. That's less time wasted.

Mrs. Jenkins doesn't spend time grading papers for writing errors when students write to learn. "I only comment on their papers regarding their use of information," she said. "My comments are pretty much limited to 'How do you know?' and 'Get more specific'."

Furthermore, students often work in pairs or small groups to review each other's work. "The students frequently do comment on each other's papers. Students who are taking the time to write about a problem want to get it right," she said.

Using These Activities in Your Classroom

In this chapter you saw examples of how math teachers can use writing through

- narratives that involve math,
- real-world applications often involving role playing,
- peer dialogues on paper, and
- problem solving that involves writing.

As is true of most learning, the math learner goes through a process of focusing, gathering data, organizing, and drawing conclusions. Since this process needs time to evolve around any one problem, a written record of the thinking process guides the learner in the process and gives him or her a chance to review what happened in reaching the conclusion.

The following note-taking guidelines help to structure the written record of the thinking process, thus making it easier for students to see what they are doing and to clarify their processes in the future.

The Issue: What is the question I want to answer?

The Data: Can I visualize the setting of this problem or list the data I need to work out the solution?

The Functions: What guidelines or formulae will I need to analyze the data? Do I have to look up anything?

The Resolutions: What reasonable explanations or answers can I now give to my initial questions?

Further Questions: What do I want to know that will help me work on future problems like this one?

BECOMING MORE SPECIFIC

Definitions and Reviews

In general, teachers in all subject areas, from history
and literature to psychology and biology, have found
that when students write about course readings, lectures,
discussions, and research materials they understand
better what they know, don't know, want to know—and
how it all relates to them.

(Fulwiler, 1987, p. 6)

Extended definitions, book reviews/reading
letters, and peer evaluations reinforce learning
in Claudia Reeves' seventh- and eighth-grade
language arts classes. We suggest ways in
which reflective/expressive writing can be
used for other subject areas.

If you believe that students are turned off by writing, then I wish you could have accompanied me to Mrs. Reeves' language arts class.

Students were engrossed in writing, talking about writing, and editing writing. Students waited in line impatiently for their turn at the word processor. After Mrs. Reeves introduced me to the class and explained I was collecting student writing samples that demonstrated *Writing Is Learning*, students rifled their notebooks, folders, and legal pads for writing samples they wanted me to read. In minutes, I had collected a tall stack of poems, short stories, book reviews, compositions, and extended definitions.

I must have had a quizzical expression on my face, because Mrs. Reeves said, with a wide smile, "As you can tell, my students are not very shy about their writing."

As you'll see, the kinds of writing done by Mrs. Reeves' students can also be used in all school subject areas. These activities, like those discussed in Chapter Two, increase learning by intensifying and prolonging students' interaction with subject matter. They also sharpen students' skills in analysis and communication.

Even in English class, not all student papers are graded for grammar, spelling, or writing style. As Mrs. Reeves explained, "Sometimes you just want students to think about a topic or problem."

Mrs. Reeves went on to explain the purposes for which she uses writing to learn: "I use writing activities to check for understanding, as a way to revise instruction, and as instructional strategies. Writing helps the students learn, and it helps me learn what they're learning and how well they are learning."

Extended Definitions

"This week the class is writing extended definitions. I especially like these papers because they help students build a body of knowledge and give students practice in skills of organization," she said. Mrs. Reeves' guidelines and study aids for extended definitions are printed at the end of this chapter.

Extended Definition: Courage

Purpose: To help students become independent learners and practice research and organization skills when they develop multiple perspectives of an idea or concept.

Prompt: Define the word *courage* in your own words. Give a dictionary definition, list synonyms and antonyms, describe a symbol related to courage, describe one incident of courage in your life, and give a quotation using the word *courage*. (See guidelines at end of this chapter.)

Evaluation: Check for understanding and accuracy.

Student Writing Sample

Courage

Courage is a word that means (in my own words) standing up to things, forces, or even people that threaten and scare you. It means never backing up when your back is to the wall. People who have courage are usually people who have it easier in life.

The dictionary definition of courage is "the quality of mind or sprit that enables one to face danger with confidence; resolution, and firm control of oneself; bravery; valor." A couple of synonyms would be fearlessness, heroism, daring, and gallantry. I think that best fits the description. An antonym of courage would be cowardice.

Once when I was about five years old, at Kindercare (my kindergarten), a little girl fell and banged up her knee, while running inside for a snack-break. Almost by instinct, I ran, picked her up, and told the teacher she needed help. I got a medal for showing courage, and some candy. To this day it still feels like "instinct" to help someone who is hurt.

A good symbol of courage would be a flag, with the words "courage forever" on it. In the middle of the flag, there would be a warrior with his weapons, and a little snake by him. Another good symbol would be two lions, with a shield separating them from one another.

Sir Thomas Browne once said "where true fortitude dwells, loyalty, bounty, friendship, and fidelity may be found. That is courage."

Julie Cavanaugh

Students can pack an impressive amount of information into five short paragraphs! Five perspectives on *courage* are included in Julie's extended definition: her everyday definition; a dictionary definition; synonyms (what else is like courage); antonyms (what words describe the opposite or absence of courage); symbolic representations of courage; and how another writer describes courage. The process of researching and describing these multiple perspectives of courage not only reinforces learning but also helps ensure that students develop fully rounded understandings of this important concept. The real-life incident that Julie selected to exemplify courage demonstrates her solid understanding of the concept.

For contrast, let's see how the writing process helps another student learn the *limits* of her understanding of a concept.

Extended Definition: Paradox

Student Writing Sample

Paradox is a word that most people don't know the meaning of, much less use in everday conversation. People don't even realize it, but sometimes they are even a paradox. Let me put it this way, a paradox is something (or someone) that says one thing but means another.

A dictionary defines a paradox as "someone or something with apparently contradictory or inconsistent qualities or facets," and that is a good definition, I guess, if you can understand it. In other words, you can never tell what they/it will be like.

If you've ever seen Back To The Future (Part 1), you should know what a paradox is. In the movie, a time paradox occurs Marty McFly's mother falls in love with Marty.

I pretty much understand what one is, because I once had a teacher that was a prime example. "Mrs.Smith" would be all nice and cheery to everyone, and then BANG!, she'd turn into the Wicked Witch of the West. Also, one of my good friends had an excellent point when she said to me, "Sarah, YOU'RE a paradox!" The more I thought about it, the more I realized it was true. I mean, no one, not even myself, can tell what I'll be like.

The thesaurus gives synonyms like: mystery, enigma and ambiquity, but the only one a seventh grader would have a clear understanding of is mystery, so that doesn't help. It's easier to use antonyms because a paradox is anything but clear, known, or understandable.

"Jane Doe" is someone who could be used as a negative definition of a paradox. She never talks, (and I mean never) she's always on time, on task, and always does what's expected of her. To me, that's a little monotonous, but if that's the way she wants to be, it's fine with me. If I were told to pick a symbol to represent a paradox, the only thing that would be appropriate would be a huge question mark. Since a paradox is a mystery, I think it fits.

I'll leave you with the words of an unknown and not-so-famous person. "If you go around trying to find a paradox, there's no doubt you'll find one, for YOU will cause it."

Sarah Koenitz

Sarah's extended definition shows how she struggles to blend her understanding of paradox with the expert's definition. Students teach themselves when they write extended definitions.

I had fun "listening in" as Sarah searched for a definition of *paradox* that would satisfy herself and her reader. In her search, Sarah discovered words such as *enigma* and *ambiguity* that she rejected as too complex for a seventh-grader to understand. Overall, Sarah seemed more confident about what a paradox *isn't*. Do you think Sarah would gain a better understanding of *paradox* if a future extended definition focused on *ambiguity* or *enigma*? Would that be para-doxical?

Extended definitions can be used in any subject area to help students develop research and organiza-tion skills and gain broad understandings of ideas and concepts and their applications. Teachers can change the prompt to fit the writing topic, and they might want to drop the antonym component or replace the symbol component with a description of a concrete example.

Social studies teachers can encourage students to read newspapers and news weeklies when extended definitions are assigned for words such as *democracy, justice, equality, war,* and *freedom.* Extended definitions can be used for more concrete words, such as *recall, felony, misdemeanor, referendum, probation,* or *immigration.*

Teachers of physical science and life science can use extended definitions to develop multiple perspectives on *evolution, population, health, genetics,* or *rain forests.* Art teachers can formulate prompts for extended definitions that develop students' understanding and appreciation of *composition, form, texture, Impressionism,* or *perspective.*

Extended definitions can personalize learning. As Sarah's writing sample shows, students enjoy writing about subject matter when they get to write about themselves at the same time. I was beginning to understand why Mrs. Reeves' students were so enthusiastic about writing.

Natural and Unthreatening

Mrs. Reeves discussed her approach to student writing:

I let students write in ways that are natural for them. That's what makes writing unthreatening. Students know ahead of time what papers will be graded for mechanics. Those papers, however, are never graded on the first draft. The graded papers all go through a review and editing process before they are 'finally' handed in. At the end of the marking period, students select what papers they want to be graded on. So mechanics are emphasized, but not on every paper. For the most part, the remainder of the writing in class is to foster thinking and learning. The writing also keeps me informed of what students are doing and how they are thinking.

I have found that students write more freely when the instructions are clear and complete, and when they have a real-life audience for their writing. Book reviews, for instance, are written as letters to me.

Book Reviews/Reading Letters

Like most English teachers, Mrs. Reeves assigns book reviews. In her class,

- students select the books they read from a list of recommended titles;
- book reviews are written as letters, *not* plot summaries;
- students are often required to read each other's book reviews and comment on them.

"In their book reviews—we call them reading letters—I want to see the students focus on one particular aspect or incident of the story they are reading," Mrs. Reeves explained. "I want them to make interpretations and extrapolations. I want to see that they know what things MEAN—to the text and to the real world. This helps them become conscious, critical readers. This kind of interaction with text comes easier when students read books that they selected on their own."

Donald Vesta, whose language arts class we'll visit in Chapter Five, uses a similar activity to reinforce students' outside reading. In his class, students read and write about stories in magazines and newspapers. "In addition to reinforcing themes and topics we're studying, this kind of reading helps expose students to a variety of writing styles in the real world," Vesta says.

Book Reviews/Reading Letters

Purpose: To encourage students to read critically, interpret information, apply information.

Prompt: See guidelines at end of chapter.

Evaluation: Check for understanding, accuracy, and reading progress.

Student Writing Sample

I am reading *Fallen Angels* by Walter Dean Myers. It has 307 pages and I'm on page 161. This book is about courage. Perry could have got himself killed when he planted the mine pointing the wrong way. If he didn't have some of the luck he has had he would be dead quick. Usually in real life you can't make some of the mistakes he is making. Luckily one of the Vietnamese turned the mine back around thinking that he was pointing it at Perry when he was really pointing it at himself. Perry was so scared when he set the mine that he didn't pay any attention to where he set it. Although you have to give him some credit. I think it may be a little scary setting a mine in pitch black with VCs all around you. When the Vcs found them Perry was to scared to shoot anyway. He kept seeing things that had to do with dying. Peewee was shooting the Vietnameses heads off!

Charlene Webster

In her reading letter, Charlene did an outstanding job of identifying the book's theme, contrasting characters, discovering how events in the book are related, and making connections between the text and her own experiences. Let's look at another reading letter, and then we'll examine and discuss Mrs. Reeves' comments on her students' writing.

Book Review/Reading Letter
Student Writing Sample

Dear Mrs. Reeves,

I am reading *Endangered Species* by Franklin Dixon. This book has 152 pages and I am on page 61. It is about poaching.

There is a man named Jellicoe in this book. I don't like him very much because he was snooping around the boys too much when they were doing their investigating. Like, little things happen when he puts a gun to the boy's back and pretends to be a poacher poaching people, and then says, "Just seeing if you boys were awake." That kind of thing is not needed in investigations.

If I was an English teacher, I would definatly share this book with my class because it adresses one of our worldwide problems now. Animal Endangerment! The class would need to know about this kind of thing and it has real-life happenings.

Like when the ranger saw a dead cheetah which had been shot by a poacher and almost caught the man.

This book is not as good as Mr. Dixon's other books. It was harder to get into, but now it's getting better.

Kyle Anderson

Of course, students in any discipline can learn more about a subject area when they read "outside" the textbook and write about their reading. Outside reading is not limited to books. Students can read newspapers, news magazines, and general interest magazines for stories related to a particular topic or field of study. Filmstrips, film documentaries, movies, puppet shows, theater productions, songs, and art exhibits can be found that deal with specific themes of educational value.

Reading letters can be adapted to fit many different situations. Prompts can be formulated by teachers to steer students to the most beneficial aspects of the experience, or students can be asked to simply recall and interpret one part of the experience and extrapolate from it.

Teacher's Comments

It's interesting to contrast Mrs. Reeves' comments on the reading letters by Charlene and by Kyle. In the margin of Charlene's letter, Mrs. Reeves wrote, "Good job of reflecting on one incident. Please return (this paper) to me." In the margin of Kyle's reading letter, Mrs. Reeves wrote, "You are a *mature* reader—and need to read more difficult books for the most part!" At the end of Kyle's reading letter, Mrs. Reeves wrote: "Have you read many Gary Paulsen books? Try *Woodsong*—it's nonfiction and talks a lot about his outdoor experiences with animals. I loved it!"

In Charlene's case, Mrs. Reeves is supportive and accepting. In Kyle's case, she's less accepting but still supportive. She compliments Kyle as being a mature reader before suggesting he tackle more difficult texts. At the end, she makes a personal connection with Kyle's interest in the outdoors as she recommends a more difficult author.

"My job is to encourage reading, not discourage reading. Still, I want to see the students challenging themselves," Mrs. Reeves explained to me.

Like many teachers who use *Writing Is Learning*, Mrs. Reeves prefers to coach students, not to criticize or berate them. Comments are helpful and friendly; they praise as well as guide. Reprinted below are comments she made on students' reading letters to reinforce study and writing skills or to point students in new directions of thought. Comments such as these represent suitable responses for teachers in all subject areas:

To a student discussing a book about the desert:
"Good job of concentrating on one or two examples from the book. Is there anything about the desert you would like—either to live there or to visit?"

To a student describing a "weird" character in a book:
"Do you think he would be your friend?—or would you avoid him?"

To a student describing a murder mystery:
"You are focusing on the art and technique of the book—then you are giving specific examples! Can you run another copy of this (reading letter)? In darker print? I'd like to keep it."

Here are some responses to student writing from teachers in other subject areas. They're similar to Mrs. Reeves' responses in tone, substance, and purpose. These teachers' comments stay focused on students' use of information, not writing style.

"This is very true. Can you think of an example from one of our recent studies showing how these three religions have made an impact on the world?"

"What is the definition of Holocaust? Great detail. Good point."

"Back then writers didn't think this was wrong. What are your feelings when you read about prejudice? This would be a good place to use an example from the book."

"I'm glad you were able to see this point."

Of course, the following comments mentioned by Mrs. Jenkins in Chapter Two are perennial favorites among teachers in all subject areas:

"Get more specific!"

"How do you know this?"

Comments such as these don't take long to write. Teachers use such comments to acknowledge students' efforts, challenge students to deeper reflection, and give students the individualized guidance that gets educational results.

Donald Vesta and other teachers report that they skim students' papers, looking for key words or phrases, and write comments as necessary.

Peer Review and Response

Claudia Reeves, Carol Jenkins, and other teachers use peer review and response sessions in conjunction with reflective/expressive writing. Peer review sessions eliminate significant amounts of time that teachers would otherwise spend on reading papers.

In addition to saving teachers' time, peer review and response sessions increase the amount and quality of students' manipulation of facts and concepts. As Mrs. Jenkins said, students "want to get it right" when they write about facts and concepts for an audience of their friends. Also, students become active learners—not passive listeners—when they read and talk about each other's subject-area writing. As one social studies teacher told me: "Students learn more from group discussions than from group listening." Importantly, students at all levels of academic achievement can contribute and succeed in peer review and response activities.

Protocol for Peer Review and Response

Here's how Mrs. Reeves conducts peer response sessions in her eighth-grade language arts class. Throughout the semester, students independently select literature to read and review from a list of recommended reading. (Teachers in other subject areas might let students read magazine articles and newspaper stories or watch films or videos dealing with recommended instructional themes.) Students write their reviews, focusing on one or two questions that prompt them to give their reactions to the story. (These prompts will be considered more fully in the discussion of "Twenty (Better) Questions" in the next section.) Teachers in other subject areas can develop their own lists of questions and review formats that would be more appropriate for their respective subject areas.

Periodically, Mrs. Reeves collects the reviews and distributes them to groups of students. Each student reads four or five reviews and critiques them for content and conformity to Mrs. Reeves' guidelines. Students write their comments on the back of the reviews and initial their comments. "That way, I know who is saying what," Mrs. Reeves explains. "It also lets me check off in my book which students are fully participating in the review sessions." She collects these papers and reviews them to find out which books students are reading, how closely students are reading their books, and how attentively each student is commenting.

Mutually Reinforcing Skills

The peer review process requires students to use several mutually reinforcing skills. Students must read their books closely to write reviews that discuss critical aspects of literature, as suggested by the list of questions discussed in the next paragraph. Then, as peer reviewers, students must formulate and defend questions and comments about other students' books and book reviews. Whether they are writing or reading the book reviews, students practice the skills of analysis, evaluation, and argumentation. They also learn about the themes, characters, settings, and plots of many more books than they could independently read in a semester.

"This process took a few semesters to perfect," Mrs. Reeves said. "I found that giving each student a list of questions and the reading letter guidelines really helped. Also, I let students look at examples of exemplary reviews. I've learned it really helps to give students examples of what I want them to do."

Mrs. Reeves uses ideas found in the article "Twenty (Better) Questions" by Kris L. Myers (1988). In this article the author points out that, instead of pop quizzes, students are asked to keep journals in which they "respond first to their perception of the work (what it means), then to the connections and associations within them that caused the affective response." (Myers, 1988, pp. 64–65) Mrs. Reeves' reading letter guidelines and Myers' list of "Twenty (Better) Questions" are given at the end of this chapter.

Myers points out that these responses can be graded "on seriousness of intent and obvious knowledge of the story. Unlike answers on the objective pop quiz, responses are impossible to fake; the reader knows immediately whether the student has read and thought about the work." (1988, p. 65) The author also finds that students benefit from this approach:

Yes, more of my students are reading their assignments more of the time. They *do* see response writings as a positive reward. But more than that, they see themselves as critics and meaning-carriers. They are less intimidated by and more intimate with the printed word. The mystery in the text has become the mystery in them. And that is a mystery they want to solve. (Myers, 1988, p. 65)

Actual Student Responses

The following peer responses to reading letters show that her students have little trouble staying on task, even when they work in small groups. These responses show that even eighth-grade students can be highly critical readers, although some might benefit from greater tact as critiquers.

> This [review] sounds like a summary of the book. You did not include your thoughts and feelings and you also did not support any thoughts if you had them. Did you even read this book? J.H.
>
> No supporting details No examples from the book Are you really reading this book? R.O.S.
>
> Who are your characters. What are their problems. What is the plot. C. M.
>
> A little bit of a summary, but it sound like you are reading the book and enjoying it.rww

Are these students ready for a quiz on the elements of literature or the elements of an exemplary book review? Do these students have a good understanding of how to read literature? Will these understandings affect they way they write their own short stories, poems, and book reviews/reading letters? You'll find that students in your classes can soon become equally critical readers of each other's subject-matter explanations and applications when you provide frequent and friendly opportunities for students to use their knowledge in this collaborative learning activity. Peer review and response can be used in any subject area when students write to learn.

Using These Activities in Your Classroom

The illustrations in this chapter showed you how to construct writing activities that maximize student learning while minimizing the teacher's load by using

- personal definitions,
- reading letters or book reviews, and
- peer-review sessions.

In many respects learning means becoming more specific. To grow in knowledge, an individual either adds detail or finds a way of pulling together many details under an umbrella, under a generalization. Adding detail requires focusing, sharpening definitions, or taking a different perspective. Pulling details together for young learners usually starts with a personal reaction, for example: "I found those actions acceptable because_____."

To guide students in becoming more specific in their learning, ask them to divide a piece of paper into three parts and to make notes as they reflect on these three questions:

1) What is my present perception, view, or understanding?

2) What needs clarifying or what is fuzzy in my understanding?

3) How can I apply this idea or book to my life or to the world around me?

Whether they are defining an important term or are gathering their thoughts to write a book review, those three guiding questions give them direction and information for writing to learn.

On the following pages are the questions, forms and guidelines that were referred to in this chapter.

Twenty (Better) Questions for Your Reading Letter

Keep this paper in the reading section of your binder.

You may use one or more of these questions to help you write a response to your reading.

1. What character(s) was your favorite? Why?
2. What character(s) did you dislike? Why?
3. Does anyone in this work remind you of anyone you know? Explain.
4. Are you like any character in this work? Explain.
5. If you could be any character in this story, who would it be? Explain.
6. What quality(ies) of which character strikes you as a good characteristic to develop within yourself over the years? Why? How does the character demonstrate this quality?
7. Overall, what kind of feelings did you have after reading a few paragraphs in this story? Midway? After finishing the story?
8. Do any incidents, ideas, or actions remind you of your own life or something that happened to you? Explain.
9. Do you like this piece of work? Why or why not?
10. Are there any parts of this work that were confusing to you? Which parts? Why do you think you got confused?
11. Do you feel there is an opinion expressed by the author through this work? What is it? How do you know this? Do you agree? Why or why not?

12. Do you think the title of this work is appropriate? Is it significant? Explain. What do you think the title means?
13. Would you change the ending of this story in any way? Tell your ending. Why would you change it?
14. What kind of person do you feel the author is? What makes you feel this way?
15. How did this work make you feel? Explain.
16. Do you share any of the feelings of the characters in this work? Explain.
17. Sometimes works leave you with the feeling that there is more to tell. Did you feel this way about this story? What do you think might happen?
18. Would you like to read something else by this author? Why or why not?
19. What do you feel is the most important word, phrase, passage, or paragraph in this work? Explain why it is important.
20. If you were an English teacher, would you want to share this work with your students? Why or why not?

(Myers, 1988, p. 65)

Form for Reading Letter

Date Due _____

I am reading (title of book - underlined) by (author). It has (number) pages, and I am on page (number). This book is about (one word).

Finish your letter by using the following guidelines:

- Try to write a whole page.

- Do *not* write a summary of what is happening in your book.

- *Do* write about your thoughts and feelings about the book.

- Be sure to support or explain your thoughts or feelings by using specific examples or incidents from the book.

- Use "Twenty (Better) Questions" to get ideas for writing your letter. Respond to no more than 2 or 3 questions in one letter.

- Do *not* try to write this letter in class. Write your letter for homework so that you can think about it and read over it to make sure that it makes sense.

- Use the model to help understand how to do this.

- Sign your name!

Guidelines for Extended Definitions

After you have chosen a topic, enter it on the "Information Gathering Sheet" below. Then fill out the rest of the sheet. Begin with a dictionary definition; then pick and choose from the other categories until you have gathered enough information.

Information Gathering Sheet

Subject of Extended Definition: _____

    Dictionary definition

    Synonyms and antonyms (Thesaurus)

    Negative definition (a statement of what the subject is not)

Extending with Connotative Meanings (Personal Details)

    Your personal definitions and feelings

        Sensory details:

        Memory details:

        Reflective details:

Other people's definitions (Your mother or father? a classmate? a policeman? a songwriter? a senior citizen? your best friend?)

Quotations (Famous people, literature, songs)

Symbols (objects used to stand for the subject)

Additional stylistic devices: simile, metaphor, irony, repetition, alliteration

_____

Name   Date   Hour
_____

Name _____

Checklist for Writing Extended Definition Essay

IDEA DEVELOPMENT

*___ ___ 1. State the topic (abstract noun you select) in the first paragraph.

___ ___ 2. Early in the paper, establish the main point about the topic, the purpose for the paper, and awareness of the audience.

___ ___ 3. Use your own voice; avoid sounding like an encyclopedia report.

ORGANIZATION

___ ___ 4. Work on introduction and conclusion to make them interesting.

___ ___ 5. Use transitions to avoid a paper that sounds like a list.

___ ___ 6. Group details in a logical manner and check constantly to make sure that your paper makes sense.

___ ___ 7. Check for paragraphing that reflects grouping of details that go together.

SUPPORT

___ ___ 8. From the "Information Gathering Sheet" choose several details that support your main point.

SENTENCES

____ ____ 9. Vary length and beginnings of sentences.

____ ____ 10. Check for run-on sentences and fragments.

WORDING

____ ____ 11. Clarify definitions or quotations that are difficult to understand; restate in your own words.

MECHANICS

____ ____ 12. Check for correct spelling, punctuation, and capitalization at the editing step of your paper.

____ ____ 13. Write legibly in ink or type final draft so that it will be easy to read and will reflect your pride in your work.

* The first of the two spaces is for the writer to check as he or she writes the first draft. The second space is for the writer and reviewer to check at the revising and editing stage.

ORGANIZING INFORMATION

Summaries

I learn from writing when I take notes. This helps me because it's easier for me to understand something when I see it on paper. You also learn from writing when you take a paragraph and put it into your own words.
(Teddy Wilson, student)

Students recall and analyze information when they write reading summaries and learning summaries of topics and study units. Students develop observation skills and multiple perspectives when they write from the future. Note taking also increases learning.

Students don't have to be academic leaders in order to benefit from opportunities to write about their studies. In examining students' work, I'm often struck by the extremes in writing skill and learning achievements among students in the same class.

Reading Summaries

What also strikes me is how hard students think when they write, regardless of their class standing or writing skills. Here's one of my favorite student writing samples: It's a seventh-grader's summary of information covered in a textbook reading assignment.

Reading Summary: Roads

Purpose: Students recall, analyze, and demonstrate comprehension of a body of facts when they state the main points of a reading assignment.

Prompt: List the main points of the reading assignment.

Evaluation: Check for accuracy and comprehension.

Student Writing Sample

They found raw materials and finished products. They went over land by horse or horse drawn wagon. The roads where narrow and rough. They had dirt paths. They traveled slow and uncomfortble. Rain made roads muddy. John L. McAdam developed a road of crust stone it made transportation faster. By 1830 Great Britain completed a system of inland waterways.

Neil LeJeune

I'm fond of this summary for several reasons. When I read it, I think I can feel Neil struggle to keep "putting one sentence after another," as Zinsser described the writing process. I think I can hear Neil asking himself as he writes: "Have I said enough? What more do I know? How can I keep going? Am I making sense?" I like this sample because it shows how Neil kept thinking and writing until he had said all he knew or all he wanted to say.

I like Neil's summary for another reason: It made me ask, "Is this child gaining anything by writing about information he reads in his social studies text?" I'm not certain Neil understands that "finished products" are produced, not found. My first response to this summary was that its style and content are not exemplary.

However, when I reread this summary and focused strictly on the information it contains, I got a different impression of Neil and of his writing. He identified finished products and raw materials; modes of transportation; characteristics of road construction; John L. McAdam; McAdam's important application for crushed stone and its implications for transportation; and a system of inland waterways completed by 1830. Neil described the relationship between weather and road construction and how they combined to affect travel convenience, comfort, and speed.

Neil's summary actually contains much information from the reading assignment. It also confirms what researchers have discovered: Students don't have to be exemplary writers to benefit from writing activities. (Copeland, 1982) Neil can use his informative summary as a study aid, regardless of the fluency of his writing style.

Here's another reading summary, from world history student Robert Gnatt.

Reading Summary: Decline of Feudalism

Purpose: Students must recall, analyze, and demonstrate comprehension of a body of facts when they state the main points of a reading assignment.

Prompt: List the main points of the decline of feudalism as discussed in the text.

Evaluation: Check for accuracy.

Student Writing Sample

Feudalism started to decline in the 1200's. Some of the things that lead to the decline of Feudalism are; the feuds between nobles and weakened, there was no need for knights because people were using new weapons such a gun power, the stone castles that the lords lived in wouldn't stand up against the power of the cannons and the cities became wealthier and under control and so many of the laws were not needed, and the people trained in government took over the jobs of vassals.

> As you can see there are tons of things that lead to the declining of feudalism, and there are so many more. The process of declining was ended in the 14th Century.
>
> Robert Gnatt

There is a "ton" of information about the decline of feudalism in this reading summary. Robert has clearly given some thought to his reading and is able to identify some of the salient factors in feudalism's decline. I like his emphasis on cause and effect and the way he carefully framed his discussion historically, citing the beginning and ending centuries of the decline of feudalism. Despite the amount of information, his teacher could easily and quickly skim Robert's summary to check for accuracy.

Reading summaries are popular because they are brief, direct restatements of learning; they economize on both time and words. Student writing focuses only on subject matter learned, ignoring real-life applications or personal speculations. Written discussion is minimal when students simply "state the main points" related to a topic or concept they studied. Consequently, summaries are quickly written by students and easily skimmed for accuracy by teachers.

More Practice Writing Summaries

Although reading summaries are easy to skim quickly, they are intellectually demanding because they require students to think critically and exercise judgment. Students must identify, analyze, and compare and contrast information in order to select the most important facts. For this reason, many of my college students reject summaries as important aids to reading comprehension. They say they are afraid they will leave out important information when they write reading summaries. (Wills, 1993) This fear among college students could suggest that students at all grade levels need to write more—not fewer— reading summaries to gain skill and confidence in identifying critical information about a topic or concept. As Charles, one of my engineering students, complained: "The summary as a form of reading comprehension [exercise] does not make sense to me. I have to first be able to understand the information in order to summarize it." Indeed, Charles, that's the *main reason* for writing a reading summary in the first place!

Learning Summaries

Learning summaries are popular because they require students to review and select the main points of a study unit or semester, not just one reading assignment or classroom activity. Mrs. Jenkins uses learning summaries in her math classes at the end of each marking period. She asks her students to name one skill or concept they learned in the grading period and list the main points about that concept or skill. Other teachers require learning summaries more frequently during the semester. Here's a learning summary from Mrs. Jenkin's class, written by student LaDonna Sears.

Learning Summary: End of Grading Period

Purpose: Students recall, analyze, and demonstrate comprehension of a body of facts when they state main points of a concept, topic, or activity.

Prompt: Name one thing that you learned in Math during the first grading period. Thoroughly explain the concept.

Evaluation: Check for accuracy.

Student Writing Sample

One of the things we learned was to graph. There were three types, the line graph which shows change over time, circle graph which shows parts of a whole and all sections total 100, and the divided bar graph which is used to compare amounts.

My favorite is the bar and circle, the line is kind of hard. I mostly used the bar graphs since it compaired data. Bar Graphs contained a title, two axes, appropriate vertical scale, key and stacked bars (add data together).

That is one thing we learned this grading period.

LaDonna Sears

LaDonna does a good job of recalling the three types of graphs the class studied—line, circle, and bar—and summarizing their differences. She carefully lists elements of a bar graph and describes (parenthetically) how to create a stacked bar graph. Her summary makes me think that she learned other things in addition to graphs in the grading period.

Summarization is easily adaptable to a variety of writing formats. At the end of each school year, Donald Vesta asks his English students to write letters to their parents in which students summarize their learning. Although the summaries look like letters, the writing purpose is summarization of the year's instruction. The length of many of these letters (several were more than 300 words long) forces me to include only excerpts from them. In the examples printed below, see if you can detect how these students' tone and use of detail indicate how much they enjoy this opportunity to review and validate their learning for an important audience: their parents.

Learning Summaries: Letters to Parents

Purpose: Students recall, analyze and demonstrate comprehension when they select main instructional points from a semester of study.

Prompt: Write a letter to your parents that summarizes what you learned about writing this year.

Evaluation: Check for accuracy.

Student Writing Sample (Excerpt)

Dear Mom and Dad,

This year all we do is write . . .

Usually we start by brainstorming for ideas and when we get one we identify the audience that will be reading it. Then we find the purpose of writing the piece. The reason we are writing this is to inform you of how we write. I usually get assigned the type of writing but most of the time I get to choose the topic. My favorite type of writing is a letter form, because it helps me realize their is an audience reading my paper and it makes me write so that they understand what I am writing about. Right before I start my rough draft I figure out the appropriate tone and voice . . .

Kelly Court

Student Writing Sample (Excerpt)

Dear Mom and Dad,

. . . Our teachers, to help us improve as writers, have taught us the Writing Process. The Writing Process is the process that people use to write. It includes prewriting, making a draft, revising, editing, and finally, making the piece public. Most people do this whenever they write, but being aware of this process may help in making a piece better.

I have many goals for myself as a writer. I feel that with enough experience I will improve enough so that I become at least a proficient writer. Even during the past few months, I think that I have improved immensely . . .

Eric Raymond

Student Writing Sample (Excerpt)

Dear Donna and Dad,

Through my growth as a writer, I have learned many distinct ways of expressing my feelings and perceptions. . .

I have now found why it is important to complete each element from the writing process: prewriting, drafting, revising, editing, and publishing. Mastering the five elements of the writing process has also allowed me to blend some techniques of writings into my papers. I have been able to recognize my point of view, use figurative language, description, etc., and I have been able to identify my purpose and audience . . .

Tara

I like the way Kelly took care, in the fifth line of her summary, to state the purpose of the letter she was writing. She describes nicely the kinds of decisions that writers must make before they start writing. I also like Eric's concise listing of the steps of the Writing Process. I chuckled when he said his goal is to become "at least a proficient writer." I think he already is. Tara's letter shows an especially focused and mature analysis of her writing skills, processes, and finished products.

Skimming through learning summaries composed by students is a quick and easy way to find out what your students have learned. These letters show that Donald Vesta could justifiably be proud of the semester's instruction about writing. Summaries, though, don't have to be reserved for the end of the semester. Summarization is teacher-friendly writing that helps students prepare for a weekly quiz or end-of-unit test.

Teachers can skim learning summaries and comment briefly about accuracy. Because summaries are short and to the point, they are especially well suited for peer review and response sessions. Peer review of summaries lets students compare their understandings and provides students with repetition in identifying the main points of a topic, concept, study unit, or semester.

Field Notes from the Future

Sometimes students—and teachers—need a change of pace in classroom routine, a change that doesn't stray so far from subject-area learning that it becomes difficult to get back on track. Field notes from the future are fun to write and read. They also require students to adopt a different perspective—an important aspect of critical thinking—toward objects we all take for granted. Students learn to look more closely and follow different logical paths of interpretation when they write from some time in the distant future, as the following samples demonstrate. See if you can guess the "ancient objects" described in these field notes from the future.

Field Notes from the Future

Purpose: Sharpen students' skills of perception and
analysis, foster an awareness of different interpretations and perspectives.

Prompt: You are an archaeologist in the year 2092
and you dig up an ancient object from the year
1992. Describe what you find and explain to
your peers how the object was used in 1992.

Evaluation: Optional.

Student Writing Sample

This ancient object was probably used
to aid elderly people in walking. The
wheels on the bottom make it easy to
push around, and it's adjustable handle
depending on the size the person was. The
attatched bag was used for personal
belongings. there was a button you could
press, and it made a peaceful humm that
kept you awake. This probably was
invented by someone who had trouble
walking and needed something to lean on.

Brian Richards

Student Writing Sample

I have discovered an ancient plastic case with windows in it! Inside the case is a plastic magnetized spool of tape. The purpose of such a device is the subject of great speculation. My colleagues suggested that it might represent some sort of religious object us in ancient worship rites. I have suggested that because of the spool inside, it might represent some primitive method of duplicating voice patterns or projected images. Of course, this seems too primitive to be believable, but I still suggested it as a possibility . . .

Stephanie DeMotte

Stephanie's field notes continue for another half-page in which she speculates about the importance of a label on her ancient plastic case that reads "F.B.I. Warning."

These descriptions and speculations regarding an upright vacuum cleaner and a videocassette show that there is always an element of fact in fantasy. More importantly, students must seriously apply skills of observation, analysis, and open-mindedness to write even humorous and fictional accounts. I like the way Brian identified the important features of an upright vacuum cleaner and invented a new and credible purpose for each feature. I also like the fresh eye that Stephanie brings to a videocassette. Indeed, a videocassette does have "windows" in it.

Teachers who want to use similar writing activities to reinforce skills of observation, analysis, and critical and creative thinking can easily identify tools or objects from any subject area that can be analyzed and described from the future. Maps, calculators, musical instruments, barometers, scales, graphs, charts, word processors, pencils, newspapers, and telephones are just a few of the objects of instructional importance that students can scrutinize, analyze, and interpret when they write from the future.

Note Taking

The value of note taking should not be minimized, especially when it is used in conjunction with textbook reading. Research indicates that students who take notes from their reading usually learn more than do students who simply respond to short-answer study questions at the end of the chapter. (Langer and Applebee, 1987) There is a simple reason for this: Students tend to look for the key words or phrases usually contained in short-answer study questions, and they often ignore all other information not related to the questions they are answering. On the other hand, when they are not given clues as to "what is important" or "what the questions are about," students' notes usually contain *more* information than is called for by the study questions. Lawrence Osborn's notes on feudalism, printed below, help to illustrate this point.

Note Taking: Feudalism

Purpose: Students record information for memorization and review.

Student Writing Sample

People were divided into groups and had duties

Clergy (religious leaders) - teach Christianity and help the poor and sick

Nobles - govern, enforce laws, protect the people

Townspeople & peasants - farmed and provided service for nobles based on ties of loyalty and duty.

Vassal - gave loyalty to a lord, lord protected vassal - act of homage (Knelt down), if vassal died son took over

If lord was captured vassal had to pay a ransom for a person's release

Nobles lived in a manor house (wooden building for protection).

palisade (high fence) in case of attack

1100's manor houses were made of stone and called castles

Knights were heavily armed men carried on war horses

Lawrence Osborn

Lawrence's notes contain a wealth of information, despite their casualness. Imagine how many short-answer questions Lawrence's teacher would have to create to address each relationship and bit of information contained in these notes. Whenever I'm stumped by a student's poor performance, I ask to look at a few pages of the student's notes. You can bet that student's notes are neither as comprehensive nor specific as Lawrence's notes on feudalism.

Focused Freewriting

Focused freewriting is just what its name describes: Students write freely on a topic for a period of time without concern for grammar, spelling, organization, or any of the other considerations that tend to inhibit student writers.

What emerges from a focused freewriting session on a topic or concept is a written record of your student's stream of consciousness associations and information. Such an exercise is ideal for developing students' awareness of prior knowledge and experiences about a topic when teachers begin a new study unit.

Purposes for Using Focused Freewriting

Use focused freewriting often during the semester to help students identify topics for more directed writing activities. The records of students' thoughts and associations often suggest starting points for further inquiry and for more polished writing. These teachers report that focused freewriting helps students get started when they aren't sure what they want to say. In Chapter One we saw that a student produced a 5,000 word essay in a freewriting exercise that focused initially on one brick in a building.

Focused freewriting can be used to reinforce instructional goals and themes. Each semester I begin my technical-report writing class with a focused freewriting project. Students and I write for two minutes, describing the instructor's chair. Then we each read our descriptions to the class. This gives me a good sense of each person's awareness of form, function, stress loads, joinery, materials, coatings, and other aspects of physical reality important to engineering students and to technical writing. Students are often surprised to learn how differently other people look at the same chair. The diversity of details that are noticed about my chair helps to demonstrate the richness and complexity of the physical world as well as the complexity of systematic observation and accurate description. This focused freewriting introduces and dramatizes an important instructional theme: Nothing is obvious to everyone.

Focused freewriting also allows students to discover new meanings and new interpretations. Earlier this year, I had an opportunity to introduce a freshman English class to 'The Flight of Aeneas', an important part of Virgil's *Aeneid*. I used focused freewriting in this lesson because I couldn't think of any other way—except for lecturing—to get across the point about this part of the poem that I wanted to make. Fortunately, one student, Nicholas Isaac, was in class that day to get the discussion flying in the right direction.

The students had read this complex section of Virgil's epic poem the night before. In class discussion we established that the action centered around the main character Aeneas and his family members: his mother, father, wife, and son. We talked about Aeneas' responsibilities toward his family that convinced him to lead his family to safety outside of town while he really wanted to stay in town and fight the Greeks. During the flight, however, Aeneas' wife Creusa got separated from the group and was killed by the Greeks. When Aeneas discovered that Creusa was missing, he returned to town—only to be met by Creusa's ghost which, in a lengthy monologue, surprisingly upbraids Aeneas for grieving his loss.

I divided the students into three groups and asked them to talk about this surprising conversation between Aeneas and his wife's ghost. I then asked the students to write their thoughts about the poem and their discussion of it.

While the students talked, I stood at the front of the class and waited for something to happen. I knew I was taking a risk.

Students in group two talked heatedly for a while about the responsibilities Aeneas felt to his wife, Creusa. Then one student, Nicholas, dropped out of the group discussion and started thumbing through the text and writing feverishly. I walked over to see what was happening. Nicholas had half a page of thoughts written when he laid down his pen, looked up at me, and said: "You know, his wife felt she had important responsibilities to the family, too. After she was killed, her ghost said to Aeneas that she felt she had to sacrifice her life so everyone else could get away from the Greeks and stay alive. Her ghost said she didn't mind, it was just the way things had to be."

I asked Nicholas to repeat his points to the rest of the class. The other students agreed immediately, and added their own comments: Aeneas, the warrior, was not the only hero in this part of the poem. The students concluded that Aeneas' courage was no greater than Creusa's: Creusa died uncomplainingly while her husband and son escaped. The bell rang too soon. The students left the class still talking about the poem.

I didn't grade the students' focused freewriting; in fact, I didn't even collect the papers. One student's thinking through freewriting had produced the insight and discussion I had hoped for. Had I lectured all afternoon, I would not have excited the kind of interaction with the poem for the whole class that Nicholas accomplished when he was allowed time independently to read, talk, think, and freewrite with a focus.

Essays

Announcing an essay assignment in class typically brings a round of groans from students. However, essays are too valuable a learning exercise to be shelved because students "hate to write" and teachers "don't have time to grade essays." What teachers and students mutually hate about essays, principally, is grammar: getting grammar right while writing and making grammar correct while grading. This situation is unfortunate, because few writing activities compete with essays for allowing students to bring together a variety of facts under one heading and discovering their interrelatedness, as Joanne Radakovich does in this essay.

Essay: Social Classes

Purpose: Students synthesize facts related to a general topic and discover these facts are interrelated.

Prompt: Write an essay explaining how the Industrial Revolution affected social classes in Great Britain.

Evaluation: Check for accuracy and comprehension.

Student Writing Sample

Essay: Social Classes

Until the Middle Ages, in England there had been two major social classes. The upper class were the nobles and the lower class were the peasents. Rich Merchants were a middle class that developed later. The rich merchants grew in numbers and even grew richer during the Industrial Revolution a lot of the factory, railroad, and mine owners became as wealthy as the nobles. After the revolution some middle class families started to spend weekends at seaside resorts, which were easier to reach now that railroads were common. That is what the Industrial Revolution did to the social classes.

Joanne Radakovich

Joanne demonstrates in this essay that she can identify and relate a variety of facts that, combined, led to the emergence of the middle class. I like the way she was careful to set the historic stage for these changes with a concise description of social organization in the Middle Ages. I like the way she identified critical developments of the Industrial Revolution that, combined, changed England's social structure. I like her awareness of the causality between economic change and social change. I think this essay shows Joanne is well prepared for a test on this material. I also like the fact that, when used to foster learning (not to demonstrate it), essays don't have to be corrected for writing errors.

Here's an essay from Raul Martinez, a seventh-grade social studies student. I've printed enough of it for you to see how it alternates between subject matter and Raul's personal beliefs and experiences, synthesizing both realms of knowledge.

Essay: Conflict

Purpose: Synthesize facts and interpretations.

Prompt: Write an essay about a conflict between two groups of people. Be sure to explain differences in beliefs that led to the conflict.

Evaluation: Check for accuracy and understanding.

Student Writing Sample

My conflict is Christian/Romans. This conflict happened because of differences in beliefs and not knowing about the other group.

My topics are; Differences that caused the clash and What was the clash like. I am going to mention these two topics in my report.

First of all, the Romans started this persecution around 64 A.D. and it continued for 250 years. During this persecution, the Romans tried to weaken the Christian Religion, but it actually got stronger. It did this because people were dying and hurting for what they believed in. In the tough times the Christians stayed together and gained new believers.

But you can't say the Christian were perfect. The Romans did have a partial reason for this persecution. The Christians did things like criticize Roman holidays and festivals. They also refused to hold a public office. Because if they held a higher office, they could get observed as a god. And they wouldn't agree with that considering their philosophy, everyone is created equal. The Christians criticized the festivals & holidays because of the way the they were held and what they were about. They also tried to get the Romans to adopt Christian festivals . . .

Raul Martinez

Do you think Raul is prepared for a quiz or exam on the Christians and the Romans from A.D. 64 to A.D. 400? Has Raul internalized an understanding of social conflict that will be useful in subsequent social studies units or in making sense of events and attitudes in his neighborhood—or the world?

I like Raul's attempt to blend new information about Romans and Christians with his preexisting world view. I sense this writing assignment about conflict has Raul feeling—conflicted. I think Raul, with this essay, is just beginning to understand the complexities of conflict, change, and difference. I don't think the end of this essay signals the end of Raul's reflection. Had Raul's teacher felt hesitant about assigning essays that take valuable time to grade and correct, Raul might have missed this important opportunity to express, and work on, his new understandings.

Using These Activities in Your Classroom

Summaries and essays both demand a sense of organization in order to convey meaning in succinct form. Summaries pull together information as presented. Essays present personal interpretations of a topic or a series of events.

To guide students in the formulation of summaries, suggest that your students use a narrative framework for organizing the information they have read or heard. The basic narrative framework shows who did something and its subsequent results. To modify that notion for summaries, encourage your students to practice writing summaries that consist of three sentences. Each sentence consists of a response to these types of questions:

1. Who or what is involved in a central way?
2. What happened or what occurred?
3. How is this situation concluded or resolved?

This practice activity merely gives students a sense of direction in the writing of summaries and should not be seen as a formula that restricts thought or limits the dimensions of summarizing.

In a similar way, essays can be guided through directing questions like the following:

1. What are the important ideas involved in this discussion?
2. Why am I interested in these ideas or events?
3. How do I give meaning to these events or resolve the ideas in my own mind?

These guidelines will give students an initial framework that provides some security as they gradually branch out into more complex summaries and reactions.

121

SUMMING UP

Letter Writing

Writing helps me understand who I am because sometimes (not all the time) my writing reflects me.
(Carly Behrens, student)

Throughout this book we have shown a number of ways for students to use writing to help them learn. In this chapter we will look more closely at letters in which students reflect on their experiences in using the various kinds of writing we have been talking about. Letter writing is very "user friendly," giving students a chance to review, analyze, and integrate their learning. These letters also help the teacher discover what students are learning and how they are thinking about subject matter.

Donald Vesta and I were seated in his eighth-grade language arts classroom. The students had just hurried off to lunch, leaving desks scattered haphazardly around the room. Beneath the desks, sheets and balls of paper—the debris of thinking—littered the brown carpet.

Windowsills, desks, tables, book shelves, and other horizontal surfaces were layered with newspapers, magazines, texts, folders, and spiral-bound collections of student writing. Posters, pictures, and more student writing covered the walls. The colors of ink and paper offered a welcome contrast to the gray sleet that blew outside the long wall of tall Gothic windows.

Donald had cleared one side of a worn maple table where we sipped from warm mugs of steaming black coffee. We were talking about his class writing activities and how they increase subject-matter learning when I asked him, "What do your students think about writing? Do they believe it helps them learn in all the content areas?"

Donald squinted at me and thought for a moment. Then, his blue eyes widening with characteristic vigor, he said, "Well, hey! Why don't we just ask them? I'm curious, too, about how they connect writing and learning. In fact, why don't I just make that one of their writing assignments next week? It will be fun to find out."

Donald did ask his eighth-grade students to describe in a letter to me "How Do I Use Writing to Learn in All Subjects?" Of course, teachers in any subject area can use similar prompts to encourage students to think about they use writing to learn. Responses to questions such as "How Does Writing Help Me Learn

Biology" or "How Do I Use Writing to Learn American History" can help students identify and appreciate writing's unique contribution to learning. Responses to such prompts can help a teacher identify each student's learning style and study habits, which can help a teacher teach more effectively. I've reprinted several of the letters I received from students in Donald's class exactly as I received them. After reading these letters, I think you'll agree: Reflective/expressive writing can be fun for students and informative for teachers.

How Do I Use Writing to Learn?

One student found that writing helped with memorization and the development of new ideas:

Dear Mr. Wills,

When I write I learn a lot. Writing helps focus on key ideas. When I write notes it helps me memorize what I have written. When I am writing down Ideas it helps get more ideas by just looking at what I have written. Writing helps me express my ideas and feelings. When I am writing and I make mistakes it helps me learn punctuation. Writing really helps me with learning.

Stacy Simos

Another student showed that he understood the connection between writing and thinking:

Dear Mr. Wills,

You have asked my class to tell you how we write to learn. I am an audio/ visual learner but I like to take notes because when I do that I automatically remember it. As you write or take notes the information also goes into your mind, thats the way I look at it. When I write I think about what I am writing and some-times that opens up my mind to new thoughts and feelings. Many students think of learning as a job, but I think it's fun. I like anything that will make me think. I am a good essay writer, but I am not so good at writing short storys. I like writing essays because it makes me think about the world around me and current issues. I learn alot from writing, and I think that it should be associated with reading. We use the same alphabet, but mainly you have to write something to read it. I am glad to be a part of your study. Good Luck!

Eric Raymond

A third student stressed the value of writing in organizing thoughts and in becoming aware of what he knows:

Dear Mr. Wills,

Writing to learn is something that I don't think we are even aware of. We do it thinking of it as only an assignment but it helps us gather our thoughts into planned out explanations. Things we don't think about we can teach ourselves by writing it down. If it is needed later than it is much more easily remembered by a visual learner if he/she has an image of the writing.

Jason M. MacNeil

Finally, the advantages of writing to learn are so well described in the next letter that we saved it for last. As you read it, think about the many writing activities and student samples we've presented to support our contention that writing *is* learning.

Dear Mr. Wills,

Responding to your question of how I use writing to learn there are many ways. I use writing to analyze, memorize, study, summarize, focus on key ideas, express feelings, emotions & opinions, take notes, answer questions, record my thoughts and to clearify & organize ideas. I basically use writing to record, which helps me learn.

Felicia Martinez

As these letters indicate, writing prolongs students' interaction with subject matter and helps them focus on key ideas and information. Opportunities to produce written records can also help students with memorization. Most importantly, writing helps students go beyond memorization of facts and concepts by allowing them to use information and see how it fits with what they know and need to learn. When students are *writing* about your subject area, they are *thinking* about it as well.

Benefits to Students

As Eric Raymond pointed out in his letter, learning can be fun. It doesn't have to be "a job" that students do just because they are required to. Students can be eager to learn when they understand the importance of what they learn. Writing gives opportunities for students to blend school learning with their real-world concerns and experiences. Such activities make learning individually purposeful—and fun.

Writing fosters discovery and helps students become independent learners. They can "teach themselves," as Jason said in his letter. Because writing has to make sense, students intellectually wrestle to formulate "planned out explanations" of subject-area information. Even when writing is viewed as "only an assignment" to be completed for a grade, it helps students to gather their thoughts. The writing product gives students another way to remember important information.

These letters about writing and learning show that adolescents can have a good grasp of how they learn and how writing supports learning in all subject areas. These samples show that students are eager to write about subject matter when they understand that writing makes learning easier, more personal, and more fun.

Students, teachers, and researchers agree: Students learn more—and better—when they write about what they're studying. But aren't teachers already too busy to give more assignments, especially writing assignments? Where do teachers find the time to grade these extra papers? Are biology and math teachers expected to teach writing skills? Won't more writing turn kids off to schoolwork? How do teachers incorporate writing into unit plans already formulated? These are important questions that teachers ask us—and themselves.

The answers to these questions have been given throughout this book. The key to the success of this approach lies in the use of writing as a way of learning that allows students to think on paper, to work through problems, and to experiment with ideas; it is not meant to be used as a test, a finished essay, or a project to be graded.

These important distinctions from most school writing are implicit in the descriptor *reflective/expressive*. The word *reflective* reminds us that the purpose is to focus, intensify, and prolong student interaction with the subject matter, not to earn a grade in writing. The word *expressive* refers to the conversational language acceptable for this kind of writing. (Britton, 1975, pp. 11–18)

Benefits to Teachers

Teachers give several reasons for using writing to reinforce learning:

- Student papers aren't graded for writing skill or style. Spelling, punctuation, and grammatical errors are not corrected. Consequently, students are free to write about subject matter in their everyday language.

- When reading student writing, teachers focus on the students' use of key subject-matter information.

- Teachers don't always have to read student papers. Students can review each other's work. A benefit of peer review is that students are repeatedly exposed to facts and concepts being written about. This repetition reinforces learning.

We certainly support the appropriate use of the English language. However, when students use writing as a powerful tool to help them learn subject matter, conversational tone and grammatical irregularities are acceptable. The letters from Donald's class indicate that students can think clearly and write effectively about a topic even if they are not yet accomplished writers. This is an important point: Students don't have to be expert spellers or grammarians when they write to learn in any school subject. Consequently, students are free to give all their attention to the writing *topic*, not to their writing style.

Carol Jenkins, Donald Vesta, Claudia Reeves, and other teachers report a variety of ways in which content-area writing helps them teach more effectively and efficiently and achieve a larger number of instructional goals:

- Writing increases learning by increasing students' engagement with subject matter.

- Writing requires no special preparation.

- Writing can serve a variety of instructional purposes.

Like Vasili with his garden shovels, teachers select particular writing activities that support specific goals. Certain kinds of writing can trigger students' prior knowledge of a topic and generate interest in a new learning unit; others can encourage and support discovery learning. Students can also be given a chance to apply new learning to real-life purposes or situations and to summarize their learning, which can be especially useful in the middle of a learning unit or prior to testing.

Teachers also report that student writing can actually save them time. They find that they reteach less but do it more effectively when they monitor students'

131

progress through writing. Furthermore, studies indicate that even students with below-average writing skills become better learners when they write about what they are learning. As students' self-concepts as learners improve, so do their grades.

Using These Activities in Your Classroom

Like all the writing activities in this book, letter writing as a wrap-up for a learning event can take on any form that you desire—informal, structured, elliptical, poetic. But just as I asked some of the students I worked with to write me a letter to explain the value of writing, you can ask your students to write a letter to you explaining what valuable ideas they have learned, how their feelings have changed, where they would like to grow next, and how this learning event could be improved for future students.

As a counterpart to the letter that your students write to you, why not write your own letter to them. What are your observations about this learning event? What did you learn? How would you change it? Did the activity live up to your expectations? You may even want to kick off the student letter writing activity by distributing your own letter first.

EPILOGUE

> . . . even the least skilled jobs will require a command of reading, computing, and thinking that was once necessary only for the professions. (Johnston and Packer, 1987, p. 116)

Teachers who encourage learning through writing make an important contribution to their students' futures. In addition to helping them learn, reflective/expressive writing gives students practice in developing thinking and writing skills they will need in the workplace. Skills of conceptualizing, collecting, interpreting, analyzing, synthesizing, and presenting information are increasingly important in all jobs, even jobs that don't require a college degree.

> . . . many high school students are un-
> prepared for how basic skills are used in
> the workplace. Most of the reading, writ-
> ing, and computation in the workplace
> is used to accomplish tasks and make
> assessments. Rather than reading from
> a single text, workers must gather infor-
> mation from several sources to solve
> problems, provide services, and perform
> tasks. (Mikulecky, 1989, p. 125)

Your students would probably be surprised to learn that secretaries, salespeople, technicians, and many service personnel spend more time reading than high-school juniors do. Also, workplace reading materials are as difficult to read as high-school texts are—and sometimes more difficult. (Mikulecky, 1989)

As low-skilled jobs decrease in number, they also become more intellectually demanding. Almost one-half of the fastest-growing jobs require the skill levels of technicians, teachers, managers, engineers, lawyers and scientists. (Johnston and Packer, 1987)

Most of the writing activities discussed in this book provide students with practice in using informa-tion as they would use it in the workplace. Most work-place writing is aimed at a particular audience for a particular purpose. Workers at all jobs need skill in using information to arrive at and defend conclusions and recommendations.

The role playing discussed in Chapter Two en-courages students to collect and interpret information in order to present and defend a point of view regarding toxic waste incineration in Jonesville.

Problem solving such as the Marshmallow Lab discussed in Chapter Two provides students with practice in observation and description. Workers often need to explain events and procedures and verify and apply outcomes.

Extended definitions discussed in Chapter Three help students collect and integrate information from a variety of sources.

Book reviews and reading letters discussed in Chapter Three encourage students to read purposefully for specific information and to summarize that information for a particular audience.

Peer-review sessions discussed in Chapter Three re-inforce skills in critical reading. Peer review sessions also provide students with practice in speaking, listening, and working collaboratively. Social skills are important in a workplace that increasingly requires teamwork and team decision making.

The types of journal writing discussed in Chapter One mimic workplace logs in which workers record information and events, ask questions, and make conjectures.

Dialogue journals are similar to inter- and intra-department memos: information and opinions are exchanged to solve problems and to avoid them.

Summarization, discussed in Chapter Four, is an important and frequently used skill in the workplace. Workers constantly need to analyze and prioritize information orally and in writing.

Even field notes from the future have workplace utility. Workers are increasingly expected to be independent decision makers. Workers need to look at a situation from a variety of perspectives. Field notes from the future can help students develop multiple perspectives on a situation and think creatively about it.

Without the kinds of thinking, writing, and social skills practiced in *Writing Is Learning* activities, high school graduates "will pay a very high price. They face the bleak prospects of dead-end work interrupted only by periods of unemployment." (SCANS, 1991, p. xv)

The writing activities discussed in this book can help students avoid dead-end careers by fostering the thinking and communication skills they will need to succeed in your class, on the job, or in college.

REFERENCES

Applebee, A. N. (1984). *Contexts for learning: Studies of secondary school instruction.* Norwood, NJ: Ablex.

Britton, J., and others (1975). *The development of writing abilities.* London: Macmillan.

Copeland, K. A. (1982, Dec.). The effect of writing upon good and poor writers' learning from prose. Paper presented at 32nd Annual Meeting of the National Reading Conference, Clearwater Beach, FL. (ERIC ED 276 993)

Fulwiler, T. (1987). *The journal book.* Portsmouth, NH: Boynton/Cook.

Johnston, W. B., and Packer, A. H. (1987). *Workforce 2000: Work and workers for the twenty-first century.* Indianapolis, IN: Hudson Institute.

Langer, J. A., and Applebee, A. N. (1987). *How writing shapes thinking: A study of teaching and learning.* Urbana, IL: National Council of the Teachers of English.

Martin, N., and others (1976). *Writing and learning across the curriculum 11–16.* London: Ward Lock Educational.

Mikulecky, L. (1989). Real-world literacy demands: How they've changed and what teachers can do. In D. Lapp, J. Flood, & N. Farnan (Eds.), *Content area reading and learning: Instructional strategies.* Englewood Cliffs, NJ: Prentice Hall.

Myers, K. L. (1988). Twenty (better) questions. *English Journal* 77/1 (Jan.), 64–65.

Pirsig, R. M. (1974). *Zen and the art of motorcycle maintenance: An inquiry into values.* New York: Bantam Books.

SCANS [The Secretary's Commission on Achieving Necessary Skills] (1991). What work requires of schools. Washington, DC: U.S. Department of Labor.

Wills, H. (1993, May). Modeling study methods: Learning for students and teachers. Paper presented at Fourth Annual Conference on Teaching Academic Survival Skills, University of Cincinnati.

Zinsser, W. (1988). *Writing to learn.* New York: Harper & Row.

Effective Classroom Activities to Promote Writing

Reading and Writing across the High School Science and Math Curriculum

Contains exciting reading and writing alternatives to the textbook approach. Explore lessons on "writing to learn" in math and science: Journal writing, scientific poetry writing, and using writing to overcome those dreaded "story problems." (Sec)

T12; 132 pp.; $16.95

Writing across the Social Studies Curriculum

Provides examples of how to connect writing activities with lessons on important topics in the social studies—a writing across the curriculum approach. (Mid/Sec)

T01; 101 pp.; $14.95

Writing Exercises for High School Students

Motivates students to explore creative, descriptive, and expository writing. Introduces the young writer to all the basics of good writing. (Sec)

T04; 81 pp.; $14.95

Critical Thinking, Reading, and Writing

Encourages reading, writing, and thinking in a critically reflective, inventive way for students at all levels. Practical classroom activities make critical thinking an achievable goal. (Elem/Mid/Sec)

T03; 96 pp.; $14.95

Celebrate Literacy! The Joy of Reading and Writing

Covers the full range of language-arts skills and literature to turn your elementary school into a reading-and-writing carnival including literacy slumber parties, book birthdays, and battles of the books. (Elem)

T11; 92 pp.; $14.95

Hot Topic Guides
to help you promote writing across the curriculum.

Hot Topic Guides can be used for either a workshop or individual study.

Each binder comes complete with everything you need to put research into practice:

- Lecture overview
- Selected articles with up-to-date information
- Annotated reference list
- Ideas for classroom projects
- Step-by-step instructions

Writing as a Response to Reading
Learn how to use reading to foster the writing process, and how to coordinate instruction so that reading and writing reinforce each other.
L05; $16.00

Computers and Writing
Learn how to get the maximum benefit from using computers as you teach writing.
L33; $16.00

Writing Apprehension and the Writing Program
Help your students break through their writer's block and come to view writing as a confidence-builder.
L31; $16.00

Ways to Evaluate Writing
Become less a copy editor and more a facilitator of your student's writing with these evaluation techniques.
L47; $16.00
